JOURNALIST ACTIVIST PARALYMPIAN
SIDENT JUDGE COMMANDER CONSERVATIONIST
WOMAN NURSE ARCHITECT ACTRESS PHARAOH
TOR BOXER LAWYER CHEMIST
DOCTOR ARTIST MATHEMATIC
RALYMPIAN QUEEN PALEONTOLOGIST
SERVATIONIST BALLERINA CHOREOGRAPHER
CTRESS PHARAOH PRIME MINISTER ASTRONAUT
MODEL REPORTER OLYMPIAN ARCHAEOLOGIST
CIAN ASTRONOMER WRITER PILOT MUSICIAN
EONTOLOGIST SCIENTIST PIRATE PRESIDENT
CHOREOGRAPHER PHYSICIST BUSINESSWOMAN
INISTER ASTRONAUT PHILOSOPHER DIRECTOR
AN ARCHAEOLOGIST POET PROGRAMMER DOCTOR
R PILOT MUSICIAN JOURNALIST ACTIVIST
IST PIRATE PRESIDENT JUDGE COMMANDER
PHYSICIST BUSINESSWOMAN NURSE ARCHITECT
UT PHILOSOPHER DIRECTOR BOXER LAWYER
OLOGIST POET PROGRAMMER DOCTOR ARTIST
USICIAN JOURNALIST ACTIVIST PARALYMPIAN
SIDENT JUDGE COMMANDER CONSERVATIONIST
WOMAN NURSE ARCHITECT ACTRESS PHARAOH
TOR BOXER LAWYER CHEMIST MODEL REPORTER
DOCTOR ARTIST MATHEMATICIAN ASTRONOMER
RALYMPIAN QUEEN PALEONTOLOGIST SCIENTIST
ERVATIONIST BALLERINA CHOREOGRAPHER

ARTIST MATHEMATICIAN ASTRONOMER WRITER
QUEEN PALEONTOLOGIST SCIENTIST PIRATE P
BALLERINA CHOREOGRAPHER PHYSICIST BUSIN
PRIME MINISTER ASTRONAUT PHILOSOPHER DIR
OLYMPIAN ARCHAEOLOGIST POET PROGRAMME
WRITER PILOT MUSICIAN JOURNALIST ACTIVIST
PIRATE PRESIDENT JUDGE COMMANDER C
PHYSICIST BUSINESSWOMAN NURSE ARCHITECT
PHILOSOPHER DIRECTOR BOXER LAWYER CHEM
POET PROGRAMMER DOCTOR ARTIST MATHEM
JOURNALIST ACTIVIST PARALYMPIAN QUEEN
JUDGE COMMANDER CONSERVATIONIST BALLER
NURSE ARCHITECT ACTRESS PHARAOH PRIME
BOXER LAWYER CHEMIST MODEL REPORTER OLY
ARTIST MATHEMATICIAN ASTRONOMER WRI
PARALYMPIAN QUEEN PALEONTOLOGIST SCIE
CONSERVATIONIST BALLERINA CHOREOGRAPHE
ACTRESS PHARAOH PRIME MINISTER ASTRO
CHEMIST MODEL REPORTER OLYMPIAN ARCHA
MATHEMATICIAN ASTRONOMER WRITER PILOT
QUEEN PALEONTOLOGIST SCIENTIST PIRATE P
BALLERINA CHOREOGRAPHER PHYSICIST BUSIN
PRIME MINISTER ASTRONAUT PHILOSOPHER DIR
OLYMPIAN ARCHAEOLOGIST POET PROGRAMME
WRITER PILOT MUSICIAN JOURNALIST ACTIVIST
PIRATE PRESIDENT JUDGE COMMANDER

GIRLS RULE

GIRLS RULE

50 WOMEN WHO CHANGED THE WORLD

DANIELLE BROWN

Button
BOOKS

CONTENTS

INTRODUCTION	6
FRIDA KAHLO	8
HYPATIA	10
CHRISTINE DE PIZAN	12
AMELIA EARHART	14
BEYONCÉ	16
NELLIE BLY	18
ROSA PARKS	20
LIBBY KOSMALA	22
BOUDICCA	24
MARY ANNING	26
MARIE CURIE	28
TUAIWA "EVA" RICKARD	30
CHING SHIH	32
VIGDÍS FINNBOGADÓTTIR	34
GEORGE ELIOT	36
MALALA YOUSAFZAI	38
RUTH BADER GINSBURG	40
ARTEMISIA I OF CARIA	42
JANE GOODALL	44
ALICIA ALONSO	46
WANGARI MAATHAI	48
HELEN KELLER	50
SUSANA RODRÍGUEZ GACIO	52
LISE MEITNER	54
MADAM C. J. WALKER	56

FLORENCE NIGHTINGALE	58	AMAL CLOONEY	84
GRETA THUNBERG	60	ROSALIND FRANKLIN	86
ZAHA HADID	62	MADELINE STUART	88
MARY PATTEN	64	SOPHIA DULEEP SINGH	90
EMMA WATSON	66	ANNA POLITKOVSKAYA	92
ANDRÉE DE JONGH	68	SHELLY-ANN FRASER-PRYCE	94
JANE FONDA	70	ZHENG ZHENXIANG	96
CLEOPATRA	72	MAYA ANGELOU	98
JACINDA ARDERN	74	AUD THE DEEP-MINDED	100
SAMANTHA CRISTOFORETTI	76	SONITA ALIZADEH	102
MARY WOLLSTONECRAFT	78	ADA LOVELACE	104
DOROTHY ARZNER	80	MARIA MONTESSORI	106
MARY KOM	82	ABOUT THE AUTHOR	108
		INDEX	110

INTRODUCTION

All over the world, female decision-makers, go-getters, and trailblazers inspire with their actions, influence with their words, and get stuff done. Girls know how to rule, and have been doing so for thousands of years.

As we travel through history we find some of the strongest, fiercest women who have ever lived. These remarkable leaders thought differently, pushed boundaries, challenged outdated ideas, and achieved things that have never been done before. Across our planet and through centuries in time we encounter

politicians, pirates, peacekeepers, pioneers, activists, spokeswomen, and survivors who changed the world—and are still doing so today!

Some stepped up because they had to, some saw injustice and decided to fight back, and some had a dream and refused to let others stop them from achieving it. These women overcame incredible odds, led extraordinary lives, and were not afraid to stand up for what they believed in. They didn't do it for fame or glory—in fact, many were not appreciated in their own lifetime—

but they left their mark on the world nonetheless. Their voices still echo loudly and have paved the way for those who came after them.

Inside you is the same courage to think big, the confidence to challenge unfairness, and the strength to push through barriers no matter how tough they seem.

Like these inspiring leaders, you have a voice and you will be heard. There are no limits to how great your dreams can grow, or how much you can achieve when you keep your curiosity burning and don't let doubts hold you back.

Remember, you are never alone during the difficult times. Many other women have traveled through hardship and found a way to rise to the challenge. Lean on their stories and let them light the way. There is always, always another way around every difficulty and you will come out far stronger on the other side.

You are bold, talented, unstoppable. And when you stay true to your beliefs, you too, can change the world.

FRIDA KAHLO

Country: Mexico | **Born:** July 6, 1907 | **Died:** July 13, 1954
Best known as: Iconic artist famous for self-portraits that symbolized her life

Frida Kahlo painted raw emotion into every brushstroke. She is remembered as an icon in the world of art, who unapologetically refused to be anybody other than herself.

Frida didn't grow up wanting to be an artist. She dreamed of becoming a physician. This all changed on a gray, rainy September day when she was eighteen: traveling home from school, she was involved in a nasty bus crash and broke her spine and pelvis in several places. Physicians saved her life, but the recovery process was slow, and she would experience pain all her life. For months, she was not allowed to get out of bed, so her parents brought her an easel that she could use lying down. With the aid of a small mirror she painted herself, turning her pain into art.

Once she was well, she sought advice from Diego Rivera, a famous Mexican painter. He was impressed by her work and they fell in love. After they got married, Frida traveled around the USA with him. It was a stormy relationship filled with passion and anguish and many arguments. They tried living apart for a while, but they loved each other too much and remarried a year later.

Frida did not shy away from difficult topics in her paintings, boldly exploring things like grief, loss, and death. Around a third of her paintings were of herself and they are remarkable in their honesty. Instead of hiding her disability, she poured her emotions onto the canvas, sharing her pain with the world. She also refused to be defined by traditional beauty standards, proudly exaggerating her monobrow and moustache in her self-portraits and wearing brightly colored clothes that celebrated her Mexican heritage.

Over time Frida's health got worse, but she didn't let this stop her from attending her first solo exhibition in Mexico. She was under physician's orders to stay in bed—and she did! She arrived at the gallery in an ambulance and was carried on a stretcher to a bed set up inside the gallery.

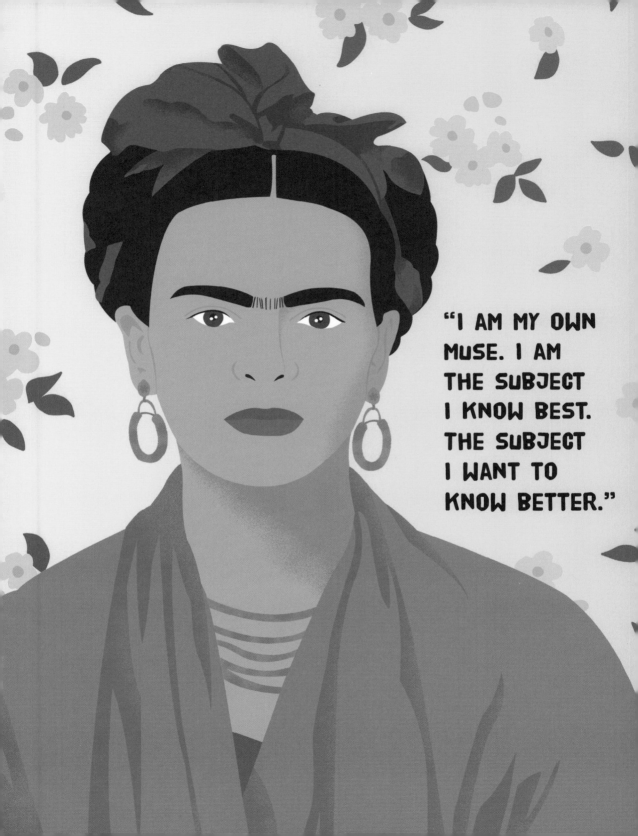

"I AM MY OWN MUSE. I AM THE SUBJECT I KNOW BEST. THE SUBJECT I WANT TO KNOW BETTER."

HYPATIA

Country: Egypt | **Born:** 350–370 CE | **Died:** March 415 CE |
Best known as: World-leading mathematician and astronomer

Very little is known about Hypatia's childhood. In fact, we don't even know when she was born! Historians have managed to narrow it down to somewhere between 350 and 370 CE, in the city of Alexandria, Egypt. She might not have been considered important at the time of her birth, but she became one of the leading thinkers of her time and her work influenced many future scholars.

In the ancient world, Alexandria was an important place of learning, famed for its enormous libraries and museums. This great city, which attracted the best and brightest minds of the day, was where Hypatia grew up. Her father, Theon, was an important scholar and he was determined that his daughter got a good education. Mathematics, astronomy, and philosophy were Hypatia's favorite subjects. She worked with her father in a school called the Mouseion, helping him update textbooks. They added notes to the works of other scholars, bringing them in line with modern thinking and new discoveries.

Soon Hypatia was writing her own books, and sharing her own ideas. She was skilled at debating, and very good at breaking mathematical concepts down in a way that made them easier to understand. She even came up with a much better method for long division. Unlike many women at the time, she also drove her own chariot.

When Hypatia knew more than her father, he retired and she took his place, becoming the first woman to lead a school. People traveled across the length and breadth of the Roman Empire just to learn from her. She taught many subjects, but was particularly well known for showing her students how to build and use an astrolabe, a special device that measures the position of the sun and the stars. Wearing the long, white robes of a scholar, Hypatia wandered the streets of Alexandria and gave lectures to anybody who wanted to listen. These drew large crowds from all over the city.

Today, Hypatia is remembered as a symbol of learning, who encouraged people to use their minds.

"RESERVE YOUR RIGHT TO THINK, FOR EVEN TO THINK WRONGLY IS BETTER THAN NOT TO THINK AT ALL."

CHRISTINE DE PIZAN

Country: Italy | **Born:** September 1364 |
Died: 1430 | **Best known as:** The most
notable female writer in medieval times

Astrologers were in high demand in
the Middle Ages. People believed they
could cure certain illnesses and predict
the future by looking at the moon and
the stars. Kings and queens across
Europe spent a fortune on the very best
astrologers money could buy. This is
how Christine de Pizan came
to France. She was
born in Italy,
but her father
was hired by
Charles V, the
king of France.
He quickly
impressed
the king with
his skills in
medicine and
fortune telling,
and his family
soon joined him
in the French
royal court. In
her new country,
Christine was
allowed into
the palace
libraries and
learned how to
read and write.

At the time, girls were expected to get married and have children and not do anything terribly exciting with their lives. Christine did get married and she had children, but her husband encouraged her to pursue her passion for poetry. After ten happy years together, he died suddenly and left her penniless. Christine did something unexpected. She became a writer.

She started with poetry, which was a big hit in the royal court. Christine soon had many patrons who paid her to write, including the queen. Her popularity grew as she explored new styles and wrote longer books. She set up a workshop in Paris, employing women to illustrate her books. Each one had to be written out by hand.

Christine was the only female professional writer in France, and she got very annoyed by the way male writers wrote about women. Girls and women were never the heroes in stories. Worse than that, they were often criticized for being too weak, or causing trouble. She believed this was one of the reasons women weren't seen as equal to men in society.

"IF YOU THINK HISTORY IS ON YOUR SIDE, LET ME TELL YOU WOMEN DID NOT WRITE THESE BOOKS. IF THEY DID, THE STORIES WOULD BE DIFFERENT."

Christine decided to do something about this. She wrote about strong women. She uncovered true stories of amazing inventors, warriors, artists, and scholars. By sharing these stories, she hoped to change the way women were treated and used her voice to call for better education for girls.

AMELIA EARHART

Country: USA | **Born:** July 24, 1887 | **Disappeared:** July 2, 1937 | **Best known as:** World-record-breaking pilot who tragically went missing when attempting to fly around the world

The first time Amelia Earhart saw a plane was at a fair when she was ten years old. She was not very impressed by the strange contraption of wood and wire, certainly not enough to want to become a pilot. This changed during World War I, when she volunteered as a nurse in Toronto, Canada, caring for injured soldiers. In her free time, she visited the nearby airfield to watch pilots fly, and when she returned home to the USA, she took her first plane ride. It was so thrilling that she wanted to learn how to do it herself.

Flying lessons aren't cheap, and to pay for them Amelia worked as a truck driver and at a telephone company. She was not a natural aviator to start with, but she got much better with practice. She bought a bright yellow plane which she named the "Canary," and soon started setting records: she was the first woman to fly at 14,000 feet (4 km), and later set a new woman's flying speed record of 181.18 miles per hour (291.5 km per hour). In 1929, Amelia helped to found the Ninety-Nines, the world's first organization to support female aviators. When she was asked why she spent so much time in the sky, she would say, "for the fun of it."

Amelia's adventurous spirit pushed her to test her limits. In 1932, she became the first woman to fly across the Atlantic Ocean by herself, landing in a farmer's field in Northern Ireland after the weather took a turn for the worst. She returned home a hero, and was awarded the Distinguished Flying Cross, a medal normally given to military pilots. Amelia wrote books about her adventures and even had a clothing line named after her. She continued to make more record-breaking trips too, flying solo from Hawaii to California and across North America.

Amelia's next goal was ambitious and infinitely more dangerous: to fly around the world. No woman had done this before and she intended to be the first. On June 1, 1937, she set off from Miami in Florida, with a navigator, Fred Noonan. Down to South America they flew, then across to Africa, and on to India and Southeast Asia. With only 7,000 miles (11,265 km) of their extraordinary journey left, they headed toward Howland Island, a tiny spit of land where they planned to refuel. They never made it. Somewhere over the Pacific Ocean their plane went missing, and despite an enormous search-and-rescue mission it was never found.

Perhaps we will never discover what happened to Amelia, but she is remembered as a trailblazer who paved the way for other female aviators and courageously followed her passions.

BEYONCÉ

Country: USA | **Born:** September 4, 1981 | **Best known as:** One of the best-selling music artists of all time

Out on the stage, Beyoncé commands entire stadiums with her powerful voice. She has transformed herself into a global icon whose music doesn't just push boundaries—it smashes them!

Beyoncé wasn't always this fearless. At school, she found it difficult to make friends and other kids picked on her. Her parents signed her up for dance classes, hoping this might coax her out of her shell. It was here that her spectacular voice was discovered and her dance teacher encouraged her to pursue singing seriously. On the stage, with everybody watching her, Beyoncé's shyness melted away and she belted out song after song. This was the moment she knew she wanted to be a singer.

At nine she started her first band, but fame and glory didn't come pouring in straight away. Nobody wanted to give them a record deal, and instead of performing in front of huge crowds they sung in a hair salon owned by Beyoncé's mother. She didn't give up: she had a dream and she was going to achieve it. Every spare minute was filled with practice, rehearsing for her big moment. Seven years later, her band Destiny's Child got their breakthrough. Their first single "No, No, No" was a roaring success and shot to the top ten in the charts. Together, the band sold millions of albums.

It was a lot of fun singing with her friends, but Beyoncé had big dreams of her own. She launched her solo career in 2003, and her debut album was wildly successful. She sings about topics that are important to her, sharing messages about independence, freedom, and, above all, the glorious power of femininity.

For almost three decades she has ruled the music industry and has won a staggering 32 Grammys—the most won by an artist ever! Still, her success isn't what sets her apart: she uses her powerful voice to make a difference and stands up for communities that struggle to get heard. Loudly and clearly, she empowers women to feel good about themselves and inspires Black women to own their culture and be proud of it.

> "I DON'T LIKE TO GAMBLE, BUT IF THERE'S ONE THING I'M WILLING TO BET ON, IT'S MYSELF."

NELLIE BLY

Country: USA | Born: May 5, 1864 | Died: January 27, 1922
Best known as: Famous journalist who became the first person in history to travel around the world

One day in 1885 a young American woman called Elizabeth Jane Cochrane read a newspaper article that said women belonged in the home, not in the workplace. Outraged, she penned a blistering response to the newspaper, and the editor was so impressed that he gave her a job. This was the start of her career as a journalist. Writing under the pen name "Nellie Bly," she soon became well known for her undercover reporting.

In the nineteenth century, people struggling with their mental health were often locked away in asylums. Nellie knew this wasn't right, so she pretended to be a patient. She spent ten days in an asylum on Blackwell Island in New York, where the conditions were even worse than she'd imagined. As soon as she got out, she exposed the horrific way patients were treated. Her story made her one of the most famous journalists of her time, and led to big changes in how asylums were run.

This wasn't Nellie's only fearless stunt. In 1872, French author Jules Verne's book *Around The World In Eighty Days* was published. It became a bestseller. Nellie decided to follow in the footsteps of the story's hero, Phileas Fogg. After studying new travel routes of the Victorian age, she told her editor at the *New York World* newspaper that she thought she could beat Fogg's time. "It's impossible," he said. "Only a man could do this." "Very well. Send a man, and I will beat him for another newspaper," she replied.

Her editor eventually agreed to send her. On November 14, 1889, she boarded a steamship bound for England and began the 25,000-mile (40,233-km) journey around the world. She traveled through Europe by train, making a small detour in France to meet Jules Verne himself. From there, she sailed down the Suez Canal and on to Asia, where she used any transport method available, including horse, rickshaw, donkey, and sampan boat. Despite the rush to keep moving, Nellie found time to do a bit of sightseeing on the way: she bought a pet monkey called McGinty in Singapore, sailed through monsoon rains off the coast of Hong Kong, visited temples in Japan, and made many friends along the way.

Nellie arrived back on US soil on January 21, 1890, and a special train sped her across the continent back to New York. Thousands of people gathered to welcome her home. Her trip took her 72 days, 6 hours, 11 minutes, and 14 seconds.

ROSA PARKS

Country: USA | **Born:** February 4, 1913 | **Died:** October 24, 2005 | **Best known as:** Activist who helped to spark off the Civil Rights movement that fought for equality for African American people

Sometimes a small act of resistance can make a huge difference. Rosa Parks courageously stood up to injustice and, in doing so, inspired other people across the USA to peacefully protest against racism.

Rosa lived in Montgomery, Alabama, which was governed by a horrible law. It was called segregation and it was designed to keep Black and white people separate. They were not allowed to go to the same schools, use the same toilets, or borrow the same books from the library. Even buses were split down the middle: Black people had to sit at the back and white people at the front.

On December 1, 1955, Rosa took the bus home from work. It was a busy day, and soon the section at the front of the bus was full. Even though she was seated in the area at the back, the bus driver demanded that she move to make space for a white passenger. Rosa was fed up of being treated unfairly, so she refused.

The bus driver called the police. Rosa was taken to jail and given a fine for her civil disobedience. Word of her arrest spread quickly, and the Black community in Montgomery, led by a minister called Martin Luther King Jr., came up with a plan. They decided

"YOU MUST NEVER BE FEARFUL ABOUT WHAT YOU ARE DOING WHEN IT IS RIGHT."

not to use the buses for as long as the discriminatory rules still stood. For 381 days, the boycott on public transport held out. Rosa helped organize carpools so that people could still get to work. Bus companies lost a lot of money because they weren't selling tickets, and eventually, the Supreme Court decided there should no longer be separate areas on public transport. Rosa lost her job and received

threatening phone calls because of her involvement in the boycott. Still, she refused to give up. Her actions showed that taking a stand could create change, and ignited the Civil Rights movement, which fought for equal rights for African American people. When she was in her eighties, Rosa was awarded the Presidential Medal of Freedom and the Congressional Gold Medal—the highest honors a civilian can receive in the USA.

LIBBY KOSMALA

Country: Australia
Born: July 8, 1942
Best known as: Winner of thirteen medals across twelve different Paralympic Games over an international career spanning 48 years

Libby Kosmala was not allowed to do PE at school. A complication when she was born caused damage to her spinal cord, which left her with no feeling in her legs. Instead, she sat on the sidelines in class. She didn't properly try sport until she was twenty, when she turned up at a wheelchair sports club—and was terrible at it! The first time she threw a discus it ended up behind her.

name to the list for the 1968 Paralympic Games. Libby was so disappointed not to be included, but Team Australia needed a secretary and they appointed her. Again, she watched from the sidelines, but it wasn't where she wanted to be. Next time, she wanted to compete.

Four years later, she went to the 1972 Paralympic Games in Heidelberg, Germany. In the early days of the Paralympics, athletes didn't specialize in one sport like they do today, and Libby competed in swimming, pentathlon, javelin, and wheelchair racing. She won a bronze medal in the swimming, but this was not the sport she would go on to excel in. Back home, she tried a new sport: shooting. Her first shot went dead center. So did her next, and her next. She had found her sport, and it wasn't long before she started winning medals against both men and women.

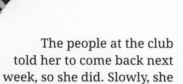

The people at the club told her to come back next week, so she did. Slowly, she started to improve, but most importantly, she began to really enjoy it.

By her mid-twenties, she was competing at the National Wheelchair Games in events including fencing, archery, and swimming. But despite dominating in her events, the organizer accidentally forgot to add her

In the 1976 Paralympic Games in Toronto, Canada, Libby won her first Olympic gold medal. Eight years later, the Paralympic Games were shared between the USA and the UK. Competing in the shooting event in Stoke Mandeville, UK, Libby won four gold medals and broke four world records!

BOUDICCA

Born: No record | **Died:** 60 or 61 CE | **Reign:** 60 CE until her death | **Best known as:** Queen of the Iceni tribe, who united the Celtic tribes of Britain and rebelled against Roman rule

The Romans wanted to conquer the world. They were making pretty good progress too. Next on their list was the tiny green island of Britannia. In 43 CE, twenty thousand soldiers landed on the southern shores, their armor gleaming and shields locked in battle formation.

At the time Britain was divided into lots of Celtic tribes, each with its own ruler. Some tribes decided to ally themselves with Rome rather than be crushed under the vast invading army. The Iceni tribe was one of these. Boudicca's husband was king of the Iceni, and for many years his people lived in peace with the Romans.

When Boudicca's husband died, he left half his kingdom to the Roman emperor, and the other half to his two daughters. The Romans were not happy. They wanted the whole kingdom for themselves and so they attacked the Iceni. Boudicca was tied to a post and whipped, her daughters were hurt, and the kingdom was robbed of its valuables.

Boudicca retaliated by raising an army. A really, really big one.

Over a hundred thousand Britons answered her call. Men and women from different tribes came together under one banner and marched on Roman strongholds. They started with the city of Camulodunum (Colchester) and burned it to the ground. Then they moved on to Londinium (London) and Verulamium (St Albans), sacking the cities and killing everyone inside. The Roman army wasn't there to stop them: they were in Wales, trying to wipe out the sacred heartland of the druids. When they heard about Boudicca's army they turned around and raced to meet her.

The Romans were led by a general called Suetonius. He ordered his ten thousand soldiers to make their stand along a Roman road called Watling Street. He chose this site carefully, as the narrow valley gave him an advantage against the superior numbers of the Britons. Boudicca and her daughters led their army into battle on chariots. Yet, even though Boudicca had the bigger army, she did not have the training, weapons, or tactics of the Romans, and she suffered a heavy defeat. Many Britons died that day, unable to retreat in the narrow valley. We do not know Boudicca's fate, though it is said that she was not killed in battle, but drank poison afterward so she could not be taken prisoner.

MARY ANNING

Country: England | **Born:** May 21, 1799 | **Died:** March 9, 1847 |
Best known as: Famous fossil hunter who made some of the most significant geological finds in history

The seaside town of Lyme Regis on the South West English coast—along with the rest of the UK—once lay deep under water. Two hundred million years later, fossil hunter Mary Anning made some stunning scientific discoveries that shaped our understanding of the planet we live on.

As a child, Mary used to join her father hunting for fossils by the cliffs near their home. When his unexpected death left the family with large debts, Mary continued to look for fossils and sold them to collectors and tourists. One day, when she was twelve, her older brother Joseph found an unusual fossilized skull. It was four feet (1.2 m) in length, with a long, pointed snout. He thought it might be a crocodile, but later Mary found the rest of its skeleton and painstakingly dug it out. It was an Ichthyosaurus, an extinct marine reptile, the first of its kind to be discovered.

When there were no fossils to be found, the Anning family struggled to make ends meet. In 1820, they had to sell their furniture to pay the rent. One of their customers heard about their plight and auctioned off his personal fossil collection to help them get by. Meanwhile, Mary's reputation as a fossil hunter continued to grow.

When she was twenty-two, she found something amazing: a complete skeleton of a Plesiosaurus. The nine-foot-long (2.7 m) reptilian creature was unlike anything seen before, and some people thought it was fake. At a special debate at the Geological Society of London, it was declared to be real, but Mary was not invited to the meeting because women, at the time, were not allowed to join the society.

Still, Mary continued her work. She taught herself about geology (the science of the earth), palaeontology (the study of fossils), and anatomy (how bodies work), and opened a small shop, selling ammonites and other "curiosities." She could often be seen combing the beaches after storms had battered the shore and exposed new fossils. The high tides and unstable cliffs were treacherous, and she narrowly escaped a landslide that sadly claimed the life of her dog, Tray.

Life was not always kind to Mary. Scientists sought her advice and bought her fossils, but she was not given proper credit for her incredible findings. Yet, her commitment to her work left a powerful legacy. The discovery that enormous

reptiles lived long before humans existed proved that the Earth was much older than people had first thought, and opened the door to a new way of scientific thinking.

Today, many of Mary's finds, including the Ichthyosaurus and Plesiosaurus, are on display in the Natural History Museum in London.

MARIE CURIE

Country: Poland | **Born:** November 7, 1867 |
Died: July 4, 1934 | **Best known as:** The first
person to win two Nobel Prizes in two
different scientific fields

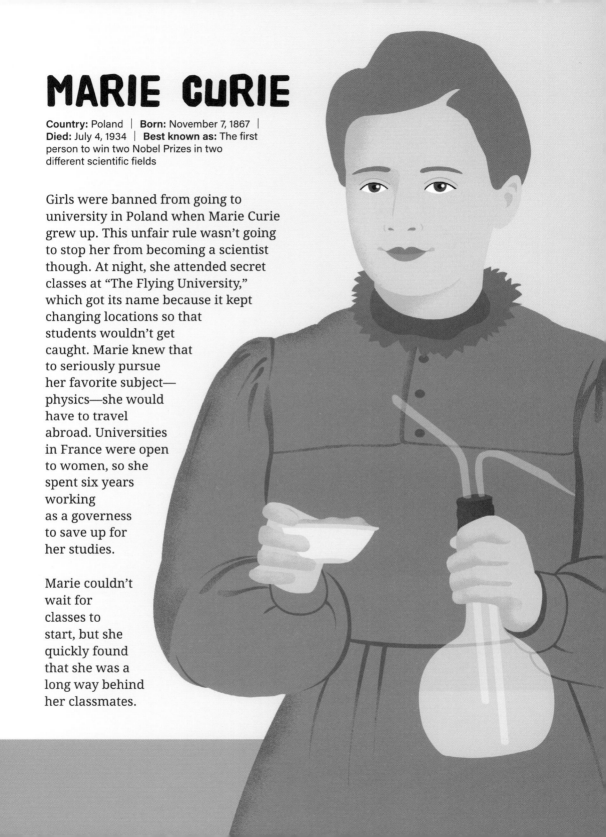

Girls were banned from going to
university in Poland when Marie Curie
grew up. This unfair rule wasn't going
to stop her from becoming a scientist
though. At night, she attended secret
classes at "The Flying University,"
which got its name because it kept
changing locations so that
students wouldn't get
caught. Marie knew that
to seriously pursue
her favorite subject—
physics—she would
have to travel
abroad. Universities
in France were open
to women, so she
spent six years
working
as a governess
to save up for
her studies.

Marie couldn't
wait for
classes to
start, but she
quickly found
that she was a
long way behind
her classmates.

During the day she studied hard, and in the evenings she took tutoring jobs to pay her way. She moved into a small apartment close to the university, and on cold winter nights she wore all her clothes to keep warm. Two years later she was top of her class, and won a scholarship to continue her studies.

When she needed a larger laboratory for her experiments, a colleague thought Pierre Curie might be able to help. He was a scientist too, and they soon fell in love and got married. Marie was fascinated by radiation, and spent hours patiently measuring the invisible rays given off by some metals and minerals. Pierre helped her, and together they discovered two new elements: polonium (named after her beloved Poland) and radium.

One day, a letter arrived in the post addressed to Pierre. He had won a Nobel Prize in physics for his work on radiation. There was no mention of Marie's contributions, so he said he would not accept the award unless his wife was included too. The committee agreed and, in 1903, she became the first woman to win a Nobel Prize. Sadly, Pierre died in a tragic accident three years later. Marie continued their work and won another Nobel Prize, this time in chemistry.

Marie wanted to use her research to change the world, and she discovered that radium helped create better X-ray pictures. During World War I, she made mobile X-ray machines so that wounded soldiers at the battlefront could be treated quicker. Her work saved many lives, but it cost Marie her own. She didn't realize that working with radiation is dangerous and it made her very ill. At the age of 66, she died. Even now, her papers are still radioactive and are kept in lead boxes. Anybody wanting to read them must wear special protective clothing.

"LIFE IS NOT EASY FOR ANY OF US. BUT WHAT OF THAT? WE MUST HAVE PERSEVERANCE AND ABOVE ALL CONFIDENCE IN OURSELVES."

TUAIWA "EVA" RICKARD

Country: New Zealand | **Born:** April 19, 1925 | **Died:** December 6, 1997 | **Best known as:** Land rights activist who fought for Māori rights

Tuaiwa Rickard grew up in a small town called Raglan. At school she was not allowed to speak *te reo*, the language of the indigenous Māori people of New Zealand, nor was she allowed to use her own name. Her teachers called her Eva.

During World War II, the government needed to build a new airfield and they decided the land in Raglan was perfect. Fifteen-year-old Tuaiwa watched as families were made to pack up their belongings and leave their homes behind. The land would be returned to them after the war, the government promised. But when the war ended, the land was not given back. It was turned into a golf course. This was the land where Tuaiwa and her *whānau* (family) had been born and where her ancestors were buried, and it held a sacred spiritual connection. Tuaiwa decided to petition parliament to get it back.

At first, the government rejected her claim, so Tuaiwa led a group of protesters to the golf course during its annual tournament. They sang songs on the ninth hole and refused to budge, even when the police turned up. Tuaiwa was arrested for trespassing and spent the rest of the day in a jail cell. All around New Zealand, people were shocked to see images of the peaceful protesters being hauled away. Tuaiwa's voice grew louder as others joined her. The government said she could buy the land back, but she turned them down. She wasn't going pay a large sum of money for something that was rightfully hers.

After many court cases, protests, and petitions, Tuaiwa won back the land. In doing so, she helped change the law: now any land taken by the New Zealand government must be returned to its original owners. For the rest of her life, Tuaiwa was committed to social justice. She worked hard to get Māori voices heard in politics, sometimes working with the government and sometimes against it when she saw unfairness. She was never afraid to speak out, at a time when many others were, and remained determined to change things. In turn, this helped many other women to be heard by their communities.

"THIS IS MORE THAN JUST FIGHTING FOR A BIT OF LAND: IT'S ABOUT BEING GIVEN THE RIGHT TO DETERMINE OUR FUTURE."

CHING SHIH

Country: China | **Born:** 1775 | **Died:** 1844 | **Years in command:** 1801–1810 |
Best known as: Leader of the largest pirate fleet in the world

In the golden age of piracy, one woman ruled the seas. Her name was Ching Shih, and she rose from the slums of Guangdong, South China, to become the most respected pirate commander in the world.

Born into poverty, Ching Shih was sent to work at the docks to help support her family. As she worked she listened to conversations, and then traded these secrets for money. When the commander of the Red Flag Pirate Fleet, Zheng Yi, met Ching Shih, he was entranced by her intelligence and beauty. He asked her to marry him, and she agreed on the condition that she was made an equal partner in his pirate fleet.

The life of a pirate was brutal and bloodthirsty: together, Zheng Yi and Ching Shih plundered towns, stole cargo from passing ships, and sold captives into slavery. Ching Shih was very good at inspiring loyalty in the crew. She created a pirate code and those who followed it were rewarded handsomely, taking an equal share of the loot. Her new rules made sure that women who were captured were not to be harmed. Any pirate who disobeyed was beheaded.

When her husband died in 1807, Ching Shih took control of the Red Flag Fleet. Under her command, it became even more powerful, growing to over 1,800 ships and 80,000 pirates. No other ships were allowed to sail in its waters without paying a hefty tax, threatening trading routes between the East and the West. The Chinese emperor decided that Ching Shih, the Pirate Queen, needed to be stopped and sent out the Imperial navy to destroy her. Ching Shih's fleet met the emperor's forces at sea and crushed them. The defeated soldiers were given a choice: pledge allegiance to Ching Shih and join her crew, or die. Many decided to become pirates, swelling the ranks of the Red Flag Fleet even more.

The Portuguese and British, unhappy that their cargo kept going missing, responded to China's call for help and sent naval ships to fight Ching Shih. Ching Shih knew she couldn't hold out forever. She agreed to step down, on the condition that she and her crew were pardoned and allowed to keep their riches. The deal done, Ching Shih hung up her cutlass and retired.

VIGDÍS FINNBOGADÓTTIR

Country: Iceland | **Born:** April 15, 1930 | **Years in office:** 1980–1996 | **Best known as:** The world's first democratically elected female president

On October 24, 1975, women across Iceland went on strike. For an entire day they refused to go to work, cook, clean, or look after their children. They wanted to prove that they played an equal role in society, and deserved to be treated— and paid—equally. It caused chaos. Factories had to close, as did many schools and shops because there weren't enough people to run them. Fathers returned home from work exhausted after taking their children with them. After that day everybody agreed: women made a very important contribution to society and ought to be recognized for it.

Vigdís Finnbogadóttir believes this strike paved the way for her to become president of her country. After the strike, things began to change and women were given equal pay. Soon there were calls for a female president and Vigdís was persuaded to put her name forward. She was an unusual choice. She didn't have a political background: she was the director of the Reykjavik Theatre Company. In the election in 1980, Vigdís squeaked a win with the slimmest of margins. Iceland had its first female elected president, and so did the world!

> **"I NEVER THOUGHT I WOULD WIN, I JUST WANTED TO PROVE THAT A WOMAN COULD RUN."**

The presidency in Iceland is mainly a ceremonial role. The country is run by the government and the president's job is to be a spokesperson, both at home and overseas. Vigdís took a keen interest in preserving the Icelandic language, which was under threat because many Icelanders learned English instead. Vigdís believed that if a country loses its language, it loses a piece of its history and, with her encouragement, it began to make a comeback. She was very proud of her culture and liked to share it with others, often traveling abroad with a cook so people all over the world could try Icelandic cuisine.

Vigdís was so popular that she was elected again and again and again. After sixteen years, she decided it was time to step down and let somebody else have a go. When she left office, she took with her another world record: the longest-serving elected female head of state of any country.

GEORGE ELIOT

Country: UK | **Born:** November 22, 1819 | **Died:** December 22, 1880
Best known as: One of the most famous authors of the Victorian age

George Eliot's name wasn't George Eliot at all—it was Mary Ann Evans. But people remember her by the name she chose to put on the front cover of her books.

Mary Ann was very intelligent, so her father sent her to boarding school to get an education. He worked on a big country estate and she loved visiting him there so she could spend hours reading in the great library. Her education came to an end after her mother died and, at sixteen, she moved back into the family home to take care of her father. In her spare time, Mary Ann joined a group to discuss political, philosophical, and religious ideas. These new ways of thinking were very different to the strict lessons she'd learned at school, and she began to question her own religious beliefs.

For fourteen years, Mary Ann cared for her father and when he died she wasn't sure what to do next. Her friends took her on holiday to Switzerland, and she decided not to come home straightaway. When she was ready to return to England a year later, she knew she wanted to become a writer. In London, Mary Ann got a job as an assistant editor at a publication called the *Westminster Review* and wrote thought-provoking articles about the state of society. It was through this paper that she met a philosopher and writer named George Lewes. When they moved in together it caused quite the scandal in Victorian Britain because he hadn't divorced his wife. Even her brother refused to talk to her. Mary Ann didn't care what other people thought. She and George were happy and madly in love.

George encouraged Mary Ann to write fiction. Not wanting her work to be overshadowed by her scandalous lifestyle, she chose a different name to write under: George Eliot. When her first book, *Adam Bede*, burst onto the scene it became an overnight sensation. Even Queen Victoria enjoyed it, and the famous author Charles Dickens sent her fan mail. Some of her books actually sold more copies than his did! Everyone wanted to know who the talented George Eliot was. When someone else pretended they had written *Adam Bede*, Mary Ann knew it was time to reveal her identity. She wrote seven novels in total, all under her pen name.

MALALA YOUSAFZAI

Countries: Pakistan and UK | **Born:** July 12, 1997 | **Best known as:** Education activist who became the youngest person to win the Nobel Peace Prize

When Malala Yousafzai was ten, an extreme group called the Taliban swept across the beautiful Swat Valley in northwest Pakistan, bringing strict religious rules with them. They banned people from listening to music and watching TV, and said girls could no longer go to school. Malala was outraged. Going to school was her right, and she wasn't going to let the Taliban stop her from getting an education.

Schools stayed open in defiance, so the Taliban started to destroy them. Walking to school each day was very dangerous, but Malala made the journey anyway. Whenever she got the opportunity, she spoke to anybody who would listen about how much she loved school and how important education was. She did interviews for newspapers, radio and TV channels, and took part in a documentary for *The New York Times*.

But, the Taliban grew stricter and shut down all girls' schools. The British Broadcasting Corporation (BBC) wanted a female teacher or older student to write a diary about life under Taliban rule. Everyone was too scared to do it, so eleven-year-old Malala volunteered, using a fake name to keep her safe. Her first blog, called "I am afraid," explained how worried she was that she might never go to school again.

After a lot of fighting, the Pakistani army pushed the Taliban out of the region and life returned to normal. Malala continued campaigning for girls' rights and was given awards for it. When she collected the National Youth Peace Prize from the prime minister of Pakistan, she asked him to rebuild schools and create a university for girls in the Swat Valley.

Malala's work was noticed by many, including the Taliban. On October 9, 2012, fifteen-year-old Malala got on the bus home from school after finishing an exam. Two Taliban gunmen stopped the bus and fired three bullets at her. She woke up a week later in a hospital in Birmingham, UK, where she had been airlifted so doctors could save her life.

Now living in the UK, Malala and her father set up the Malala Fund to help girls across the world access education. In 2014, aged seventeen, she became the youngest person ever to be honored with a Nobel Peace Prize.

RUTH BADER GINSBURG

Country: USA | **Born:** March 15, 1933 | **Died:** September 18, 2020 | **Best known as:** Supreme Court judge who fought for gender equality

At school, Ruth noticed that boys got far more opportunities than girls. It was unfair that they got to build things, she thought, whilst girls had to learn how to sew and cook. This wasn't the only time in her life that Ruth would deal with gender discrimination. Throughout her career she faced many barriers, but she would go on to make sure that other girls would never have to fight as hard as she did.

Ruth met her husband, Martin Ginsburg, at university and they both won places at Harvard Law School. There were only eight other women in Ruth's class of five hundred students. Even so, the dean once asked them why they thought they deserved to take these places from men! When Martin was diagnosed with cancer, Ruth went to his classes as well as her own, taking notes so that he didn't miss anything during his treatment. She still finished at the top of her class.

Getting a job wasn't quite so easy. Many places turned her down because she had a young daughter at home, and they didn't think a woman would be up to the task. Eventually, Rutgers University took her on as an assistant professor, but she was paid less than the men. Ruth and other women working at the university came together to fight this—and they won.

Women all over the country were facing similar challenges, and Ruth decided to do something about it. She fought many cases on behalf of the American Civil Liberties Union, arguing against gender discrimination. Inequality affected everybody, she pointed out, not just women. She argued six cases, winning five of them, in the Supreme Court—the highest court in the USA, reserved for the trickiest cases.

"REAL CHANGE, ENDURING CHANGE, HAPPENS ONE STEP AT A TIME."

Because of her outstanding work Ruth was invited to become a judge, first on the Court of Appeals and then on the Supreme Court. Only nine judges sit on the Supreme Court, and Ruth was only the second woman to be appointed. She didn't always agree with her colleagues, writing passionate statements called "dissents" about why she believed their decision was the wrong one. When she disagreed, she wore a special collar with her robes. Sometimes her dissenting statements were so powerful that they affected future laws. Ruth served on the Supreme Court until the day she died, at the age of 87.

ARTEMISIA I OF CARIA

Country: Halicarnassus, Caria | **Born and died:** Unknown | **Reigned:** Around 480 BCE |
Best known as: A well-respected and intelligent commander in the Persian Empire

Artemisia was named after the Greek goddess of the hunt. Like her namesake, she was fearless and brave and wise.

She was born 2,500 years ago and ruled the city state of Halicarnassus, in the ancient region of Caria (now in modern-day Turkey). Greece and Persia were longtime enemies and Xerxes, the new Persian king, was out for revenge. His father had been defeated by the Greeks in the Battle of Marathon ten years before. Xerxes raised the largest army the world had ever seen and prepared to invade Greece.

Artemisia was required to send five ships of fighting men to Xerxes. There was no need for her to join her crew, but she chose to fight and quickly established herself as a brilliant tactician. Artemisia sailed with two flags on her ship: a Greek one and a Persian one. When she saw a Greek ship she flew the Greek flag so they thought she was a friend, and when their ship got close enough she attacked. The Greeks placed a bounty on her head—10,000 drachma to the person who caught her. That's almost half a million dollars today!

The Greeks were losing ground and they decided to take a stand at Salamis. Xerxes gathered his commanders.

He asked them whether he should meet the Greeks in battle at sea. One by one, his commanders agreed with this plan. Only Artemisia said no. "The Greeks are better at fighting at sea," she said. "It's better to stay close to shore and play to our strengths." Xerxes liked her honesty, but decided to go ahead with the naval attack. Even though she disagreed with the decision, Artemisia still fought in the Battle of Salamis. The Persians were lured into a trap and suffered a terrible defeat. They lost three hundred ships that day.

Artemisia survived the battle and afterward Xerxes praised her highly. He sent her a full suit of armor and said she was his bravest and wisest commander. He also asked for her advice. Should he retreat to Persia and leave his general in charge, or stay and continue to fight? Artemisia told him to return home. If Persia won, the glory was his; if they lost, the failure belonged to his generals.

Artemisia was praised by both Greeks and Persians for her intelligence and leadership. It is very unusual for a person to be spoken of so highly by their enemies.

JANE GOODALL

Country: UK | **Born:** April 3, 1934
Best known as: Conservationist
and the world's leading expert
on chimpanzees

When Jane Goodall was a child,
she read about the fictional
hero Tarzan and his amazing
adventures in the jungle. She
decided that when she grew up
she wanted to travel to Africa,
live with wild animals, and
write about them. Everybody
laughed at her except her
mother. She encouraged
Jane's dreams, fueling
her curiosity. If she
worked hard enough
and didn't give up,
then anything was
possible! When
she left school,
Jane got a job as
a secretary and
saved every
penny to pay
for her trip.

In 1960, at the age of twenty-six, her childhood dream came true. Far from civilization, in the Gombe Stream National Park in Tanzania, she began her work. Day after day, Jane hiked into the hills and watched for chimpanzees. As soon as they spotted her they disappeared into the trees and didn't return. For months she patiently waited until, one day, an older chimpanzee she called David Greybeard started stealing bananas from her tent. Eventually, he trusted Jane enough to take one from her hand, and the other chimps began to accept her too.

Rather than just observing the chimpanzees from a distance, Jane lived alongside them and made some fascinating discoveries.

She watched David Greybeard and the other chimps poke sticks into holes to catch ants and termites to eat. Until then, it was thought that only humans were capable of making tools.

Her findings shocked the scientific world, but some people didn't take her work seriously. They didn't like the way she gave the chimpanzees names and talked about their personalities. Jane disagreed. She had spent years living with the chimps and she knew she was right.

For over sixty years, Jane has studied chimpanzees. She discovered that they are intelligent social creatures with different personalities, just like you and me. They play, communicate, and even fall out with each other. Sadly, chimpanzee numbers are declining because of poachers hunting them and their forest homes being chopped down. In 1977, Jane founded the Jane Goodall Institute to try to save them. The conservation charity operates all over the world, and encourages people—no matter how young or old—to get involved.

ALICIA ALONSO

Country: Cuba | **Born:** December 21, 1920 | **Died:** October 17, 2019 | **Best known as:** Prima ballerina and choreographer

Alicia Alonso left home for the grand theaters of New York City, USA, when she was sixteen. Ever since she was nine years old she had wanted to become a ballerina, but in Cuba there were no professional dancers. If she wanted to take her ballet to the next level then she had to take a big leap of faith and try to make it in a new city, far away from home.

Always looking for ways to improve, Alicia spent hours training each day and her devotion paid off. She was invited to join the prestigious Ballet Theatre, where she stunned her teachers with her technique. She was on the brink of making it to the top when she visited a physician about her eyesight, which had started to get worse. An operation could correct it, she was told, but she wouldn't be able to dance whilst she recovered. For a year, Alicia laid in bed and listened to music, imagining herself dancing the lead part in the ballet *Giselle*. This was the role she wanted to play above all others. She practiced every intricate move over and over again in her mind, her feet flying across the stage, lighter than air. But when her bandages finally came off, Alicia still could not see properly and physicians told her that she'd never dance again.

Alicia refused to give up on her dream and returned to her training. Soon after, she received a phone call that changed everything: the principal dancer in *Giselle* had injured herself—could Alicia step up and take her place? This was her opportunity to shine. When the curtains went up, she danced every step she had practiced in her mind. The audience were astounded by her sensational performance. She was everything a ballet dancer should be: graceful, agile, and strong. Not one of them knew about her visual impairment.

Alicia was promoted to principal ballerina. As her sight got worse, she taught her partners to position themselves exactly where she needed them and used the bright stage spotlights to guide her. She got offers from all over the world, but she chose to return home to start a ballet school in Cuba, so that boys and girls there could train to be professional dancers. All the while, she continued to dance: in her seventies she was still performing solo pieces!

"I DON'T WANT MY AUDIENCE THINKING THAT IF I DANCE BADLY, IT IS BECAUSE OF MY EYES. OR IF I DANCE WELL, IT IS IN SPITE OF THEM."

"WHEN WE
PLANT TREES,
WE PLANT THE
SEEDS OF PEACE
AND SEEDS
OF HOPE."

WANGARI MAATHAI

Country: Kenya | **Born:** April 1, 1940 | **Died:** September 25, 2011 | **Best known as:** Nobel Peace Prize winner for her work on women's rights and the environment

Wangari grew up in a village in rural Kenya. Here, she explored the lush countryside where the rain fell and the plants bloomed, and collected water at the foot of a giant fig tree. As she grew older, she left her village to go to school and, later, earned a scholarship to study at a university in the USA.

When Wangari returned home, years later, she found it very different to the place she remembered from her childhood. The land around her home village was no longer rich and fertile. Huge forests had been chopped down in Kenya and turned into farmland to grow tea and coffee. Without trees protecting the land, the soil hardened and the streams ran dry. Across the country people had to walk miles to find water and were struggling to grow food to feed their families. There was no firewood to cook with, or grass for animals to graze on.

Wangari knew she had to do something about it. Her idea was simple: to plant trees. Looking after the land and helping it flourish once more would, in turn, help communities thrive. There would be fuel for fires, food to eat, and clean drinking water.

Government officials scoffed when she shared her plan. They didn't believe that citizens could make a difference, but Wangari was determined to prove them wrong. She founded the Green Belt Movement, a scheme that paid women to gather seeds in the shrinking forests, and plant them in long rows.

Green belts of trees soon sprang up all over Kenya. Over the next thirty years, over thirty million trees were planted. The ground became fertile again and rivers began to flow because tree roots bound the soil, trapping moisture in the ground. Wangari's idea spread to other countries, and inspired a United Nations campaign that has led to the planting of fourteen billion trees worldwide.

Wangari saw something that many people didn't: there is a strong connection between looking after the environment and reducing poverty. In 2004, she was awarded the Nobel Peace Prize for helping communities, particularly women, restore the environment and their livelihoods. When she found out she had won the prize, she planted a tree to celebrate.

HELEN KELLER

Country: USA | June 27, 1880 | **Died:** June 1, 1968 | **Best known as:** Disability activist who campaigned for better treatment of deaf and blind people

When Helen Keller was 19 months old, she fell ill with a terrible fever. Physicians did not know what it was, or how to treat it, and the illness left her deaf and blind. Even though Helen could use some basic signs to show what she wanted, being unable to communicate properly was frustrating. Sometimes she had violent tantrums because her family couldn't understand her.

Her parents searched for somebody who could help. The Perkins Institute for the Blind in Boston, Massachusetts, sent the family a teacher called Anne Sullivan, who traveled over 1,000 miles (1600 km) to the Keller's house in Alabama. When she met six-year-old Helen, she gave her a doll and spelled out the letters d-o-l-l in the palm of her hand. Unable to see or hear, Helen found it difficult to understand what Anne was trying to say. It wasn't until Anne ran Helen's hand under water and spelled out w-a-t-e-r that the little girl made the connection between the signs on her palm and their meanings.

Helen learned very quickly after this, picking up sign language and learning Braille, a system of raised dots that can be read with fingertips. Helen also wanted to learn to speak. This was harder, but with a lot of practice she soon mastered it too. Helen and Anne became inseparable. At school, they sat together in class and Anne signed what the teacher said into Helen's hands. Helen gained a place at Radcliffe College (now Harvard University), one of the most prestigious universities in the country. None of her textbooks were in Braille, so Anne translated each one. It was here at Radcliffe that Helen's teachers spotted her talent for writing and encouraged her. Helen's first book, *The Story Of My Life*, was published while she was still studying. A year later, she graduated with high honors, becoming the first deafblind person in the world to earn a degree.

Helen wanted to make sure that other people with disabilities could have the same opportunities as her. With Anne, she traveled around the world, speaking to audiences large and small. She campaigned for more library books to be available in Braille, and established Helen Keller International, an organization that supported soldiers who had lost their vision in World War I. Later, she rolled out programmes to prevent blindness. Helen didn't just fight for disability rights: she also campaigned for women to get the vote, and helped to create the American Civil Liberties Union, which is still protecting people's rights today.

"EVERY DAY MEANS EVERY DAY. CONSISTENCY IS KEY."

SUSANA RODRÍGUEZ GACIO

Country: Spain | **Born:** March 4, 1988 |
Best known as: Paralympic gold medallist
and doctor who worked during the
COVID-19 pandemic

In 2020, the Covid virus spread around the world. Paratriathlete Susana Rodríguez Gacio was preparing for the Tokyo 2020 Paralympic Games, but when the pandemic struck she didn't hesitate to step up to the frontline. She is an expert multitasker: as well as being an amazing athlete, she is also a brilliant physician.

Susana was ten when she decided she wanted to become a sprinter. When she narrowly missed out on making the team for the Beijing 2008 Paralympics, she almost gave up. After taking some time away to think about her future in sport, she switched to paratriathlon, a combination of running, cycling, and swimming. This was a smart move because she turned out to be very good at it. In four years she was world champion.

Outside of sport she excelled too. She first qualified as a physiotherapist and then trained as a physician. In doing so,

she became the first blind physician in Spain. Susana has a condition called albinism. This means she produces less melanin, the pigment that gives our skin, hair, and eyes its color. It can also affect a person's vision— Susana's is less than 10 percent. At work, she uses special technology to magnify her screen. In sport, she teams up with a guide who races with her and helps her navigate the course.

In 2020, Susana was planning to take a break from her medical career to make sure she was in top form for Tokyo 2020. Not only was she competing in triathlon, but she had also qualified to take part in athletics, and she wanted to win her first Olympic medal. But, 2020 did not go to plan. Spain had some of the toughest Covid lockdown restrictions in Europe. For seven weeks nobody was allowed outside their house, not even to exercise. Susana worked at the hospital, helping patients who were recovering from Covid so they were well enough to go home. After her hospital shift she squeezed in three hours of exercise, training in her apartment on a treadmill, exercise bike, and rowing machine.

Putting in the effort paid off. When the Paralympic Games were held the following year, Susanna became the first athlete from Spain to compete in two different sports at the same Games. In the 1500-meter race, she ran a personal best and came fifth. In the triathlon, she won gold.

LISE MEITNER

Countries: Austria and Sweden | **Born:** November 7, 1878 |
Died: October 27, 1968 |
Best known as: Award-winning physicist
who co-discovered nuclear fission

In 1897, the law in Austria changed: women were now allowed to attend university. Four years later, Lise Meitner took the entrance exams to study physics. For as long as she could remember she had wanted to be a scientist.

There weren't many opportunities for Lise in Austria, so after she got her doctorate, she moved to Berlin, Germany. Here she teamed up with a chemist called Otto Hahn. Women were forbidden from entering the Kaiser Wilhelm Institute where he worked, but Otto set up a small work space for them in a carpentry workshop in the basement, with its own side entrance. If Lise needed the toilet she had to go to a restaurant down the street! Together, Lise and Otto wrote scientific papers and discovered a new element, protactinium. Her work was eventually recognized by the university and she was appointed head of physics.

By the 1930s Lise was one of the best nuclear scientists in the world, but Germany was becoming a very dangerous place for her to live. When Adolf Hitler came to power, Jews across the country lost their jobs. Lise, who had Jewish heritage, continued her research into the behavior of atoms,

but she was banned from teaching. Under the Nazi regime, scientists were forbidden from traveling abroad, so in 1938 her colleagues helped her sneak out of Germany. Taking hardly any possessions with her, she fled to Sweden.

Back in Germany, Otto continued their work, but he found the results of his experiments puzzling and wrote to Lise to ask for her help. Lise had a brainwave. She realized that large amounts of energy are released when an atom is split in two: this is called "nuclear fission." It was a huge breakthrough. In 1944, Otto received a Nobel Prize in chemistry for his work on nuclear fission. Lise was excluded from the award, despite her involvement.

Lise and Otto's research into nuclear fission was used by scientists in the USA to build a nuclear bomb. Lise was horrified. She wanted to change the world for good, not destroy it, and she refused to help them. After the war, she did not return to Germany and continued her work as a research professor in Sweden. In 1997, years after her death, a chemical element was named Meitnerium in her honor.

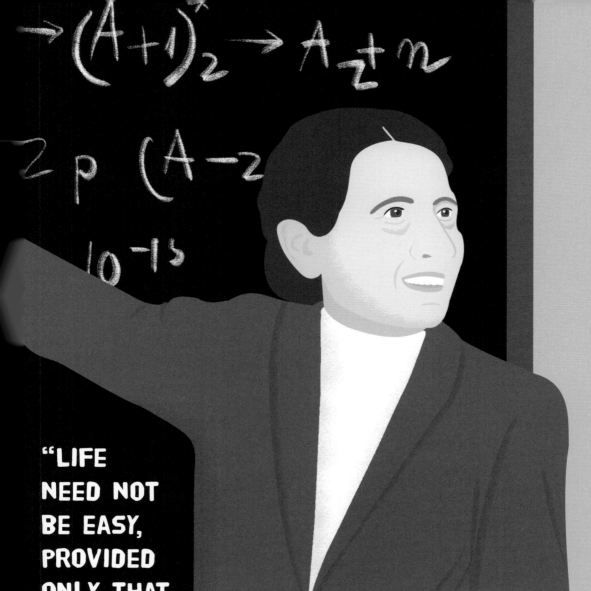

MADAM C.J. WALKER

Country: USA
Born: December 23, 1867
Died: May 25, 1919
Best known as: Businesswoman who became the first female self-made millionaire

At the age of 38, Madam C. J. Walker had $1.25 in savings. She used this to start a huge business empire that made her a millionaire. This remarkable rise to success was only possible because she dared to risk all she had and worked incredibly hard, never losing her determination to help others on the way.

Before she became a household name, Sarah Breedlove (as Madam C. J. was known back then) grew up on the cotton plantations of Louisiana, USA. Her parents had been born enslaved, as had her brothers and sister, but after the Civil War in America the government put an end to the vile practice of slavery. Sarah was born free, but life was still tough. Her parents continued to toil in the fields, picking cotton to make ends meet. Sarah worked in the fields too, and later got a job as a laundress. Before the invention of the washing machine, this was backbreaking work, but the money she earned meant she could send her daughter to school.

Sarah faced another problem: her hair kept falling out. After work, she began to experiment with different treatments for her hair, and developed her own line of products. As her hair began to grow, so did a business idea. She spent her savings on ingredients and began knocking on doors in her neighborhood to demonstrate her new hair-care regime. Now, her new business just needed a name. She found it after she married a newspaper salesman called Charles Joseph Walker, and changed her name to Madam C. J. Walker.

Orders came in thick and fast for Madam C. J. Walker's Wonderful Hair Grower. Her products were so popular that soon she needed more staff. She knew what it was like to work to the bone for very little pay, and she vowed she would never run her business that way. She started a school, which trained women to become "hair culturists," and they sold her products across the USA and beyond. Eventually, she employed forty thousand women and men.

"DON'T SIT DOWN AND WAIT FOR THE OPPORTUNITIES TO COME. GET UP AND MAKE THEM."

Madam C. J. Walker grew very rich, but she also gave back to others. She made sure her workers were well looked after, supported many charities, and gave money to fund schools. She also spoke out about the violent treatment of African American communities, and fought against racial prejudice.

FLORENCE NIGHTINGALE

Country: UK | **Born:** May 12, 1820 | **Died:** August 13, 1910 | **Best known as:** Founder of modern nursing and brilliant statistician

Florence Nightingale's parents did not want her to become a nurse. They expected her to marry a respectable man and lead a respectable life, like most young women from wealthy English families did at that time. Florence wasn't bothered about living in luxury. She wanted to help people, so, against her family's wishes, she became a nurse anyway. Victorian hospitals were filthy places, but as she worked she noticed something interesting: the cleaner the hospital, the more people survived.

In 1854, the Crimean War broke out, with Britain, France, and Turkey fighting on one side, and Russia on the other. Word soon reached Britain about the shocking conditions of the military hospitals where injured soldiers were being treated. Florence was asked to lead a team of nurses to the Crimea to see if she could make a difference, and so the women set sail for Constantinople (now Istanbul), in Turkey. Nothing could prepare them for the state of the hospital they found at the British camp. Soldiers were not dying of their wounds, but of preventable diseases caused by cramped and dirty conditions and a lack of basic hygiene. Florence set about scrubbing the hospital from top to bottom, getting rid of the rats and the fleas, and making it safer for patients.

Every evening, long after the physicians had left for the night, Florence walked around the wards to check on her patients, carrying a small lantern. Grateful for her devotion, soldiers called her "The Lady with the Lamp." She was involved in all aspects of her patients' care. She set up a proper kitchen and laundry, and also had a classroom built to keep the men's minds active. Within six months, the changes she put in place had saved many lives. Florence made a record of everything she had done, and used these statistics to change the way hospitals were run.

At the end of the war, Florence returned home a hero. Queen Victoria presented her with an engraved brooch and the British government gave her a handsome pot of money. She used this to set up the Nightingale Training School for Nurses, which transformed nursing into a proper career and championed better care for patients. Remarkably, she did most of this from her bed. She was too unwell to run the school herself, having fallen ill with "Crimean fever" in the war, but she wrote many books and papers, and continued to campaign to improve standards of nursing and hospitals.

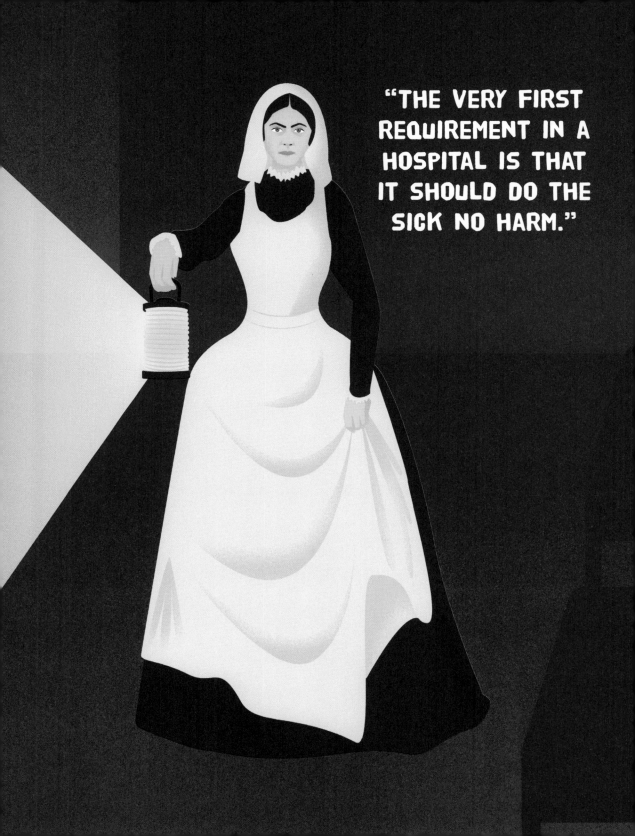

"THE VERY FIRST REQUIREMENT IN A HOSPITAL IS THAT IT SHOULD DO THE SICK NO HARM."

GRETA THUNBERG

Country: Sweden | **Born:** January 3, 2003 | **Best known as:** Environment activist who kicked off a global movement to tackle the climate crisis

Instead of going to school on Friday August 20, 2018, fifteen-year-old Greta Thunberg sat outside the Swedish Parliament. Wearing a bright yellow raincoat, she held a sign with the words "SCHOOL STRIKE FOR CLIMATE" painted in large, black letters. She vowed to turn up every Friday, until politicians did more to reduce carbon emissions.

Greta first learned about climate change when she was eight. Our planet is warming up much more quickly than it should because humans are burning fossil fuels. The gases that are released wrap around the Earth, trapping heat inside. Because of this, we are sadly seeing terrible droughts, storms, heatwaves, and wildfires. Greta couldn't understand why nobody was stopping the emissions that are causing harm to our planet and the people who live on it. Climate change affects us all, but nobody seemed to be talking about it. The hopelessness she felt caused her to experience depression. Later, she was also diagnosed with Autism and selective mutism, which meant she only talked when she thought it was absolutely necessary.

If others weren't going to act, then Greta decided she must. She started with her own family, making small changes to the way they traveled and what they ate, to lower their carbon footprint. But she realized that change needed to happen on a much bigger scale, and so she came up with an idea: a school strike. Her parents weren't happy about their daughter missing school, but they were glad she had found an important cause. Greta began her demonstration alone but she quickly gained thousands of supporters all across the world. By December, students from Japan to the UK were also calling on their governments to change the law and reduce emissions.

Her words echoed around the world. The girl who for many years found it difficult to talk now uses her voice to fight for change. When she was invited to speak at the United Nations Climate Action Summit in New York in 2019, she was determined to travel from Europe to the USA without flying. It took her fifteen days to cross the Atlantic Ocean on a racing yacht powered by solar and wind energy. At the summit, she told world leaders that they needed to do better. Some people tell Greta that young people shouldn't be activists, but she believes that each one of us can create a better future.

ZAHA HADID

Countries: Iraq and Britain | **Born:** October 31, 1950 | **Died:** March 31, 2016 | **Best known as:** Award-winning architect

Unlike many other architects, Zaha Hadid did not dream of designing tall buildings that touched the sky. Instead, she drew fantastical curves and bold geometric structures that defied the style of the time. People told her that her ideas were unbuildable, but she stood by her vision and became one of the most decorated architects in the world.

Zaha was born in Iraq. As a child, she visited the ancient Sumerian cities in the south where human civilizations built the first great cities. She was fascinated by how the land and buildings flowed together as one. At university she took a degree in mathematics, and then traveled to London to study architecture, wowing her teachers with her originality. They were so impressed that they invited her to join their architecture firm after she graduated.

It wasn't long before Zaha decided to open her own architecture firm in London. The boring rectangular buildings that shape many city skylines were too tame for her liking. She had plans to turn her own exciting ideas into real buildings. However, she faced a big hurdle. She couldn't get anybody to commission one of her daring designs. Finally, after three years of trying, she got her big break when she was asked to build a leisure center in Hong Kong. Everybody loved her explosive design that worked with the natural layout of the hillside to create an effect that looked like the building defied gravity itself. Unfortunately, Zaha never got to see it come to life because the developers ran out of money and the project had to be shelved. It was another ten years before she finally got to build her first project: the Vitra Fire Station in Germany. The building stands tall and angular, like it's ready to burst into action.

"YOUR SUCCESS WILL NOT BE DETERMINED BY YOUR GENDER OR YOUR ETHNICITY, BUT BY THE SCOPE OF YOUR DREAMS"

Soon, people wanted to build Zaha's bold designs all over the world. In 2004 she won the Pritzker Architecture Prize, becoming the first woman to be given this honor. During her lifetime she saw dozens of her ideas come to life and designed many famous buildings, including Cincinnati's Rosenthal Center for Contemporary Art, and the Aquatics Centre for the London 2012 Olympic Games. Her big ideas and courage to stick to her convictions changed the game, and redefined what we think is possible for our cities.

MARY PATTEN

Country: USA | Born: April 6, 1837 | Died: March 18, 1861 | Best known as: First female commander of an American merchant ship

Shortly after their wedding, Mary Patten's husband, Joshua, had to go away. He was the captain of a ship called *Neptune's Car* and spent long months at sea. The couple didn't want to be separated, so they decided to travel the world together. Joshua taught Mary how to navigate the ship and she assisted him with his duties as captain.

Their next voyage was to take precious cargo from New York to San Francisco. In the early 1800s this was a long journey that involved sailing down the east coast of America, around Cape Horn at the tip of South America, and back up the other side. Joshua hoped to do it in a hundred days. Mary joined the crew as she usually did, and she had some happy news. She was pregnant with their first child.

Soon, though, things started to go wrong.

The first mate broke his leg just before they left port. The ship's owners didn't want to delay the trip so they quickly hired a replacement, William Keeler, and the ship set off. The new first mate was lazy, falling asleep on shifts, and refusing to take orders. In the end, the captain locked him in his cabin to keep him out of trouble. The second mate didn't know how to navigate, so Joshua had to take over and now had two jobs to do. All this extra work took its toll, and he collapsed on the deck.

Nobody else on board could navigate, so nineteen-year-old Mary took command of the ship. Hearing the news in his cabin, William attempted a mutiny. The captain's position deserved to go to him, he whispered to the other sailors when they brought his food and water. Mary was having none of it.

"IF MY HUSBAND CANNOT TRUST YOU TO BE A FIRST MATE, THEN I CANNOT TRUST YOU TO BE A CAPTAIN," SHE TOLD HIM.

Mary called the crew together and asked for their support. They all stood behind her. Together, they sailed around storms, battled through savage seas, and cautiously steered past icebergs. When Mary wasn't out on the deck, she read all the medical books on board to see if she could find a cure for her husband, who had a high fever and had lost his vision. Finally, four months after they had set sail, a heavily pregnant Mary guided the ship into the port at San Francisco. She is credited for getting the crew home safely and keeping her husband alive.

EMMA WATSON

Country: Britain | **Born:** April 15, 1990 | **Best known as:** *Harry Potter* actress and feminist

Emma Watson sat by the telephone for hours, waiting for it to ring. She was nine years old, and she'd auditioned for the role of Hermione Granger in the *Harry Potter* movies. Before then, she'd never starred in anything other than plays at the local theater. She wasn't even sure if she wanted to be an actor when she grew up, but she had fallen in love with the character of Hermione when she read the books and desperately wanted to play the role. The phone call came when she was out of the house: she had got the part.

When filming began, ten-year-old Emma had to leave home and travel all over England. Her parents both worked full time and couldn't come with her, but she was well looked after by the crew. On top of a busy acting schedule, she and her costars also had to finish their school work and were tutored on set for five hours a day. In real life, Emma worked just as hard as Hermione. She loved memorizing lines so much that she even learned Harry's and Ron's too. The director had to keep telling her to stop mouthing them when the cameras were rolling.

Filming eight movies back to back was tough going. There came a point when Emma thought about quitting and handing over the role of Hermione to somebody else. The movies had catapulted her into global stardom at a very young age, and sometimes life could be very lonely. Now she was older, she wondered whether it was time to explore other career paths. Eventually, though, she decided to see the *Harry Potter* movies through to the end. It was an emotional moment when they filmed the last scene of the last movie. Emma had spent ten years growing up on the Harry Potter set, and now it was time to move on.

Instead of jumping straight into another role, Emma went to university to study English literature. She managed to squeeze in a bit of acting around her lectures, branching out into different roles. When she graduated from university she decided to use her platform to make a difference. She was appointed as a UN Women Goodwill Ambassador and traveled the world to promote better education for girls. In 2014, she delivered a rousing speech in the UN Headquarters in New York to launch the HeForShe campaign. This encourages everybody to work together to achieve gender equality. Men have a very important role to play in feminism, and Emma invited them to join the conversation and change the world too.

ANDRÉE DE JONGH

Country: Belgium | **Born:** November 30, 1916 | **Died:** October 13, 2007 | **Best known as:** Nurse and resistance heroine, who ran an escape route for Allied soldiers during World War II

When World War II broke out, Belgium was invaded by German forces and suffered a heavy defeat. Andrée de Jongh was working as an artist at the time, but she volunteered as a nurse to care for injured soldiers. Some of her patients were servicemen from Britain, which was one of the Allied countries fighting against Germany. Andrée quickly realized she wanted to do something to help save British soldiers and airmen who had been stranded behind enemy lines. If she could safely smuggle these men to Spain, they could return home. It wasn't going to be easy though. Spain was over 1,000 miles (1,600 km) away, across German-controlled land.

Andrée organized a network of safe houses through Belgium and France. Plenty of people wanted to help, providing food, clothes, and shelter along the way. The escape route was called the Comet Line because the smuggled men moved quickly from safe house to safe house, traveling by train, bicycle, and on foot. The entire journey could take as little as a week.

The first attempt to use the Comet Line ended in failure. Andrée sent eleven men down it, but they were arrested by police when they crossed the Spanish border. Only two made it out. Andrée decided to lead the next group herself. She took three men through occupied France, then over the Pyrenees mountains, sneaking into the British consulate in Bilbao, Spain. There, she asked British officials to help her save more Allied soldiers. At first they didn't believe that a twenty-four-year-old woman had made the journey across such dangerous territory in winter. But Andrée was very persuasive and soon secured the funds she needed.

The whole operation was very risky. Anybody caught helping was arrested. She made thirty-two successful trips, guiding 118 people to safety. On the thirty-third trip she was betrayed by a farm worker and handed over to German authorities, who interrogated her for days. She refused to reveal the identity of anybody she worked with, telling them that she was the leader of the entire operation. The Germans did not believe her, and sent her to a concentration camp where she was imprisoned for nearly two years. The Comet Line continued its work and saved around eight hundred people.

Many of Andrée's friends died in captivity, but she survived. After the war, she traveled to Africa where she worked as a nurse, caring for people with leprosy. She was given awards for her bravery, and in 1985 was made a countess by the king of Belgium.

JANE FONDA

Country: USA | **Born:** December 21, 1937 | **Best known as:** Oscar-winning actress and activist

Jane Fonda decided to follow in her father's footsteps and become an actor. He was very famous, but she wanted to get roles because of her own talent, not because she had an award-winning dad. She started modeling to pay for acting lessons, and instead of taking one class a week she did four. The year she turned twenty-three, she starred in a play on Broadway and then in a romantic comedy movie called *Tall Story*, and from there her career blossomed. Everybody wanted her in their movies, and she was given many leading parts.

Jane found fame on the big screen, but away from it she used her voice to make a difference. In 1972, she was propelled into the limelight when she visited North Vietnam, which was fighting a war with South Vietnam. The USA had taken South Vietnam's side and sent thousands of soldiers to support them. Jane spoke out against this decision and spent two weeks touring the country, calling for an end to the war. She thought if she exposed what was happening to civilians in North Vietnam it would make US pilots think twice about bombing it. This did not make her very popular at home, and some people even accused her of being a traitor.

That same year, Jane won her first Oscar for best actress in a movie called *Klute*. She went on to win many more acting awards, and in the 1980s she branched out into fitness videos, making home workouts very popular. After spending thirty years in the movie industry, she decided to take a break from acting because she wasn't enjoying it anymore. Time away helped her passion for her craft slowly regrow, and fifteen years later she made a comeback in the movie *Monster-in-Law*. Now in her eighties, Jane is still making movies. She also continues to champion many different causes, including women's rights and environmental issues.

In 2019, Jane teamed up with Greenpeace, an environmental campaign group, to launch Fire Drill Fridays. Each week, she organized a demonstration on Capitol Hill in Washington D.C. to ask politicians to act on climate change. Jane was arrested five times for protesting. Standing in a bright red coat, she refused to move until police took her away. Once she even gave an acceptance speech for a Bafta movie award whilst being led away in handcuffs! For her eighty-second birthday, Jane wanted to see if 82 friends would join her demonstration; in fact, 138 people turned up to demonstrate with her.

"IF YOU'RE A CELEBRITY, YOU HAVE A RESPONSIBILITY TO USE THAT CELEBRITY, ESPECIALLY WHEN THE FUTURE OF MANKIND IS AT STAKE."

CLEOPATRA

Country: Egypt | **Born:** 69–68 BCE | **Died:** August 12, 30 BCE | **Best known as:** The last Egyptian pharaoh and one of the most powerful women in the world

A long time ago Cleopatra ruled Egypt with her ten-year-old brother Ptolemy XIII. At eighteen, she had to deal with floods, famine, and great debt and, one by one, she solved them all. Her brother didn't like her making all the decisions by herself, however, so he got his powerful friends to force her from the palace. Cleopatra fled to Syria, where she assembled an army and prepared to invade her own country.

Meanwhile, across the Mediterranean Sea in Rome, civil war had broken out between two powerful men: Julius Caesar and Pompey. Pompey was losing so he fled to Egypt to beg for help, but Cleopatra's brother had him killed instead. When Caesar, chasing Pompey, arrived in Egypt, Cleopatra saw this as an opportunity. She knew Caesar could help her strengthen her forces and dethrone her brother, and she wanted him as an ally. However, her brother's army stood between them. Knowing she would be in serious trouble if she got caught, she smuggled herself into the royal palace rolled up inside a carpet. Impressed by her bravery and intelligence, Caesar backed Cleopatra and brought his army to help her. Ptolemy tried to escape but he drowned in the Nile River.

Egypt now belonged to Cleopatra and she made it strong. She dressed up as the goddess Isis to remind her people that pharaohs were gods on Earth. Even though she was friends with Rome, she made sure that her kingdom remained independent and it prospered under her reign. She and Julius Caesar had a baby boy together, who they called Caesarion, or "Little Caesar."

Cleopatra was visiting Rome when Caesar was assassinated. She returned to Egypt and made Caesarion her co-regent, even though he was only three years old. She would do anything to protect him, including murdering her own brother and sister so they couldn't take the throne from him.

But trouble was brewing further away from home: Rome was fighting over who should be the next emperor. Cleopatra sided with a Roman general called Mark Antony, and they fell in love and had three children together. She funded his military campaigns and led a fleet of ships against his enemy. Yet, despite her help, Mark Antony's rival Octavius grew too strong. Cleopatra and Mark Antony killed themselves instead of being captured and taken to Rome in chains.

JACINDA ARDERN

Country: New Zealand | **Born:** July 26, 1980 | **Years in Office:** October 26, 2017–January 25, 2023
Best known as: Prime Minister of New Zealand who led with kindness and compassion

When Jacinda was at primary school, she noticed some children coming in with no shoes on their feet or lunch to eat. She knew this wasn't right and wanted to do something about it. It was this memory that later inspired Jacinda to go into politics, to make a difference to people who needed it. Her aunt, Marie, persuaded her to volunteer with the Labour Party when she was seventeen, and soon she was knocking on doors to ask people to vote for the local candidate. Her enthusiasm saw her rise quickly: eleven years later she was a member of parliament, the youngest in the country. In her first speech she told the government off for not doing more about climate change.

Just before the 2017 general election, the leader of the Labour Party quit, and Jacinda was elected as its new leader. Nobody thought the Labour Party could win, but Jacinda's positive outlook and refreshing honesty made her stand out. Her party didn't win outright, but it teamed up with another party to lead the country. At the age of 37, Jacinda became New Zealand's youngest prime minister in over 150 years.

All along, Jacinda was clear about one thing: if she was to lead her country, she was not going to pretend to be someone she was not.

Time after time, she proved that a leader could be both kind and powerful. After a terrorist attacked a mosque and killed fifty-one people in the city of Christchurch, Jacinda rushed to the scene and comforted the victims and their families. Just six days later she changed the law, banning assault weapons so that this kind of attack could never happen again. During the Covid pandemic, when every world leader faced difficult decisions, she acted swiftly to shut down her country's borders and keep people safe from the virus until a vaccine was ready.

Jacinda also made history as the first world leader to take a baby to a United Nations general assembly meeting. Her three-month-old daughter, Neve, even had her own official security pass! Jacinda's modern approach to leadership turned politics on its head and redefined what a leader can be.

In 2023, after five years in charge, Jacinda decided it was time to step down. In a shock announcement, she explained that she had no more to give her country. It takes a huge amount of strength to admit that it is time to go. When she resigned, Jacinda said she wanted to be remembered for always trying to be kind.

SAMANTHA CRISTOFORETTI

Country: Italy | **Born:** April 26, 1977 | **Best known as:** Holder of the European record for the longest spaceflight

As a child, Samantha Cristoforetti watched the stars twinkling brightly over the Italian Alps and dreamt of being amongst them. One day, she promised herself, she would explore the skies.

Flying a fighter jet seemed like a good place to start, but when Samantha left school, women were not allowed to join the Air Force in Italy. So, plan B was to study mechanical engineering at university. Just before she finished her degree, the Air Force changed its rules. Samantha applied to the military flying programme and became one of the first women to be accepted. Getting her fighter pilot wings wasn't easy. Most people who start their training don't make it to the finish. It was tough on her body and her mind, but Samantha worked hard to qualify and was quickly promoted to captain.

Still, Samantha dreamed of going further and faster, and she applied to the European Space Agency. In 2009, she was chosen from 8,000 other candidates to become Italy's first female astronaut. There were lots of new skills to learn and tests to pass, and Samantha had to spend six hours at a time underwater in a spacesuit. But she was used to demanding training, and this was no different. She made every second count.

Five years later, Samantha took her first flight into space. Seeing the beautiful landscapes of our planet beneath her made her realize how insignificant human-made structures are. Fewer than a thousand people have been to space, so Samantha decided to bring space to Earth instead, by taking people behind the scenes at the International Space Station. On social media, she covered everything from what astronauts eat, to how to wash your hair in space. She also worked hard each day on her research. Astronauts spend a lot of time doing science that can't be done anywhere else, and she conducted experiments into the effect that living in space has on the cells in our body.

Toward the end of her mission, Samantha was asked to stay put for an extra month after a malfunction with a supply ship. When she returned to Earth, she had spent 199 days, 16 hours, and 42 minutes in space, breaking the record for the longest European spaceflight.

Eight years later, Samantha made a second spaceflight. This time she completed her first spacewalk, took over command of the International Space Station, and became the first person to make a TikTok video in space. Samantha took her dream and hung onto it, finding ways to keep building her skills and work around challenges to make it come true.

MARY WOLLSTONECRAFT

Country: Britain | **Born:** April 27, 1759 | **Died:** September 10, 1797 |
Best known as: Writer and philosopher who fought for women's rights

In the eighteenth century, many people in Britain and other countries thought that women weren't equal to men. Mary Wollstonecraft didn't believe this for one second. Women were smart, ambitious, and independent, but poor access to education stopped them reaching their full potential. She was sure of this, and she wanted to do something about it.

Her own education was short. While there were good schools for her brother to go to, there weren't the same opportunities for Mary: she learned how to read and write and very little else, so she taught herself other subjects. At the time, women had very limited career options. Mary opened a school with two of her sisters and her friend Fanny, but it was forced to close when Fanny died. Life, Mary realized, was too short to do something you aren't passionate about, so she decided to forge her own path as a writer.

Mary surrounded herself with philosophers who valued what she had to say and a publisher who was willing to work with her. Her big break came with the French Revolution. The people of France revolted against the king because they were suffering under high taxes and corrupt officials. When a British member of parliament criticized this, Mary wrote an article that furiously disagreed with his position. It sold out in three weeks and established her as a political writer. She followed this up with her most famous work, *A Vindication of the Rights of Woman*, which called for women to have the same opportunities and education as men.

Mary decided she wanted to go to Paris to watch the French Revolution unfold. Many of her friends warned her not to go, but she would not be discouraged. Sadly, the new regime in France wasn't much better than the old one. It sparked off the brutal Reign of Terror, and some of Mary's new friends were executed for speaking out. When France declared war on Britain, Mary was forbidden to leave the country. Worse, because of her outspoken views she was treated with suspicion. An American businessman, Gilbert Imlay, protected her by pretending they were married. Mary fell in love with him and gave birth to a daughter, but when the situation calmed down, Gilbert deserted her.

Returning home to London with her baby was difficult, but Mary continued to write and found love again with a philosopher named William Godwin. Sadly, their marriage only lasted for a few months, as Mary died eleven days after giving birth. Her second daughter inherited her passion for writing: she is better known under her married name, Mary Shelley, the author of *Frankenstein*.

"I DO NOT WISH WOMEN TO HAVE POWER OVER MEN, BUT OVER THEMSELVES."

DOROTHY ARZNER

Country: USA | **Born:** January 3, 1897 | **Died:** October 1, 1979 | **Best known as:** Trailblazing female movie director who invented the boom mic

In 1906 a violent earthquake destroyed large parts of San Francisco, USA. Shortly afterward, Dorothy Arzner's family moved from the wreckage of their home to make a new start in Los Angeles. Her father opened a café in Hollywood where movie stars often hung out, so Dorothy grew up surrounded by the big celebrities of the day. This didn't inspire her to get into movie-making. She wanted to be a physician, and during World War I she volunteered as an ambulance driver. Two years at university changed her mind: medicine wasn't the right career for her.

Dorothy moved back home and thought she'd try her luck in the movie industry instead. After visiting a studio, she decided she quite liked the idea of being a director because they got to tell everybody else what to do. Jumping straight into this position wasn't an option though: she would need to start at the bottom and work her way up. She started by typing scripts, and from there she rose to become an editor, responsible for stitching shots together so they told an exciting story. Still, she wanted to be a director so she gave the studio an ultimatum: either they give her a movie to direct, or she would move to another studio.

Dorothy got what she wanted. The studio gave her a movie to direct, called *Fashions For Women*. It was a big hit and she was asked to direct more. When Dorothy first started out, silent movies were all the rage, because the technology to record sound and play it in theaters didn't yet exist. This changed in the late 1920s, when "talkies"—films where the actors spoke—became possible. Many directors found it difficult to switch to the new format, but not Dorothy. For many years, she was the only woman director in Hollywood. Her movies starred bold female leads, and she delivered success after success in the box office. She also invented the "boom mic"— a microphone attached to the end of a fishing pole, which allowed actors to freely move about the set without heavy sound equipment getting in the way.

Seventeen movies later, she stepped away from directing, but retirement wasn't the end of Dorothy's involvement in film. She taught filmmaking at university, and made commercials.

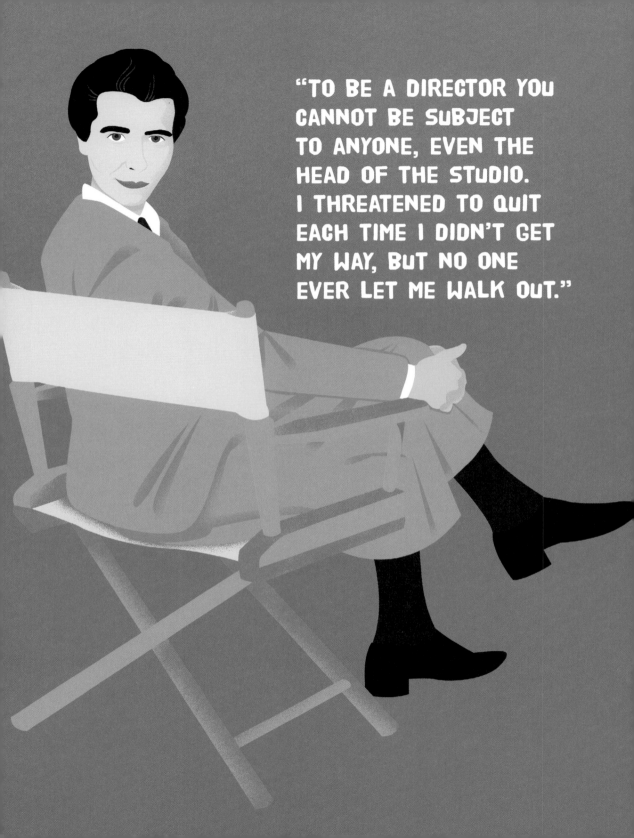

"TO BE A DIRECTOR YOU CANNOT BE SUBJECT TO ANYONE, EVEN THE HEAD OF THE STUDIO. I THREATENED TO QUIT EACH TIME I DIDN'T GET MY WAY, BUT NO ONE EVER LET ME WALK OUT."

MARY KOM

Country: India | **Born:** March 1, 1983 | **Best known as:** Six-time world champion boxer and Olympic medallist

When Mary Kom started boxing she kept it a secret from her father. Three months later he got a surprise when he saw a photo of her in the newspaper after she won the State Championships.

Mary grew up in rural Manipur, a state in Northeast India, where her family were farmers. They worked in the fields from dawn until dusk and lived in extreme poverty. Sometimes they didn't have enough food to eat. Mary was the fastest runner in her village, so at fifteen her father sent her to live with relatives in Imphal, the state's capital city. He hoped that athletics would give his daughter more opportunities to gain scholarships and a better job. Instead, she fell in love with boxing. She found a coach to train her and spent

"PEOPLE USED TO SAY THAT BOXING IS FOR MEN AND NOT FOR WOMEN AND I THOUGHT I WILL SHOW THEM SOME DAY. I PROMISED MYSELF AND PROVED MYSELF."

every spare moment in the ring. It was tough keeping up with everyone else because she couldn't afford the proper equipment or food, but she worked hard. Women's boxing was very new because for a long time they weren't allowed to compete. Many times, Mary got told she should quit.

After she won the State Championships, Mary's parents asked her to come home immediately and explain herself. They were worried she would get hurt, but

when they saw her passion for boxing they accepted it. Her mother weaved clothes long into the night so that Mary could buy boxing gloves and shoes.

Within a year, she was selected to represent India. Earning the nickname "Magnificent Mary," she went on to win medal after medal, including six World Championship titles, a bronze medal at the London 2012 Olympic Games, and gold at the Commonwealth Games.

Mary has inspired girls all around the world, by showing that it is possible to succeed in a sport that has traditionally excluded women. She also proved that it is possible to be a mother and an athlete. In 2007 she gave birth to twin boys and many people thought she wouldn't come back to her sport as strong. However, she worked hard to get back to competition fitness and the following year won another World Championship title. In 2013 she had another son, and in 2018 she and her husband adopted a daughter. Tokyo 2020 was her last Olympic Games. In 2015, Mary opened a state-of-the-art academy to train the champions of tomorrow, particularly those who come from underprivileged backgrounds.

AMAL CLOONEY

Countries: Lebanon and UK | Born: February 3, 1978 | Best known as: World-renowned human rights lawyer

Amal Clooney's family fled the civil war in Lebanon when she was two years old, escaping a dangerous conflict that destroyed many homes and displaced almost a million people. She came to the UK as a refugee and is grateful for the compassion shown to her family. Far from her homeland, she got a good education and studied law at university, first at Oxford and then in New York, USA. Specializing in international criminal law, she qualified as a barrister and represents victims of terrible human rights atrocities.

Amal made a name for herself because she doesn't take easy cases. Her clever legal arguments and courage to speak out has seen her win justice for many of her clients. She is a fierce protector of free speech, and has helped journalists who have been imprisoned on false charges to stop them from exposing the truth. She took a member of the terrorist group Islamic State to court over her crimes against Yazidis, a religious group who live in northern Iraq, and won. Governments around the world ask her to advise them on tricky legal cases. She does, but she is also not afraid to criticize them for their failure to protect vulnerable people, particularly those living in war zones.

Despite her success, Amal has never forgotten that she was once a refugee and spends a lot of time giving back. Together with her husband, actor George Clooney, she helped to fund seven schools in Lebanon so that three thousand Syrian refugees could go to school. The couple also welcomed a Yazidi refugee from Iraq into their home: he was forced to drop out of university after Islamic State sent him death threats and then destroyed his village. Amal and George gave him a place to live and helped him to continue his education at the University of Chicago.

Amal believes that together we can inspire each other to make the world a better place and ensure that future generations can enjoy the right to freedom, democracy, and equality. Standing up for what is right takes a lot of bravery, but it makes a big difference to those who need it the most.

"WE NEED YOUNG PEOPLE WITH THE COURAGE TO SAY: 'THIS IS OUR WORLD NOW, AND THERE ARE GOING TO BE SOME CHANGES'."

ROSALIND FRANKLIN

Country: UK | **Born:** July 25, 1920 | **Died:** April 16, 1958 | **Best known as:** Chemist who helped discover what DNA looks like

X-rays can uncover secrets hidden deep inside the tiniest molecules and help us understand how the world is built. Rosalind Franklin used this technology to make a very important discovery that changed science as we know it.

Rosalind started out studying coal. When World War II broke out and bombs fell from the sky, she refused to leave the English city of Cambridge for somewhere safer, and continued her research. Coal was used in gas masks to filter out poison and Rosalind's work helped to identify the best kind of coal to use, saving many lives. Still, Rosalind wanted to know more. X-rays would allow her to see inside molecules

themselves, so she traveled to Paris, France, to learn from the best scientists there. Her research was impressive and she was soon invited to join King's College in London to investigate the structure of DNA. This molecule carries information about our bodies, from what color our eyes are, to how tall we will grow. But, at the time, nobody knew what DNA looked like. Unlocking this secret would help answer questions about life itself.

Another scientist at the laboratory, Maurice Wilkins, thought Rosalind would be working as his assistant. But Rosalind hadn't come all the way to London to be anybody's assistant, and she began work with her own team trying to take X-ray pictures of DNA. It took many attempts and hundreds of hours, each failure making way for her next experiment. Again and again, she and her team bombarded DNA molecules with high-energy X-rays, improving the camera until they finally got a clear shot. They called it photograph 51.

Maurice saw the photograph in Rosalind's lab. Without her knowledge, he sent it to two other scientists, James Watson and

> ## "SCIENCE AND EVERYDAY LIFE CANNOT AND SHOULD NOT BE SEPARATED."

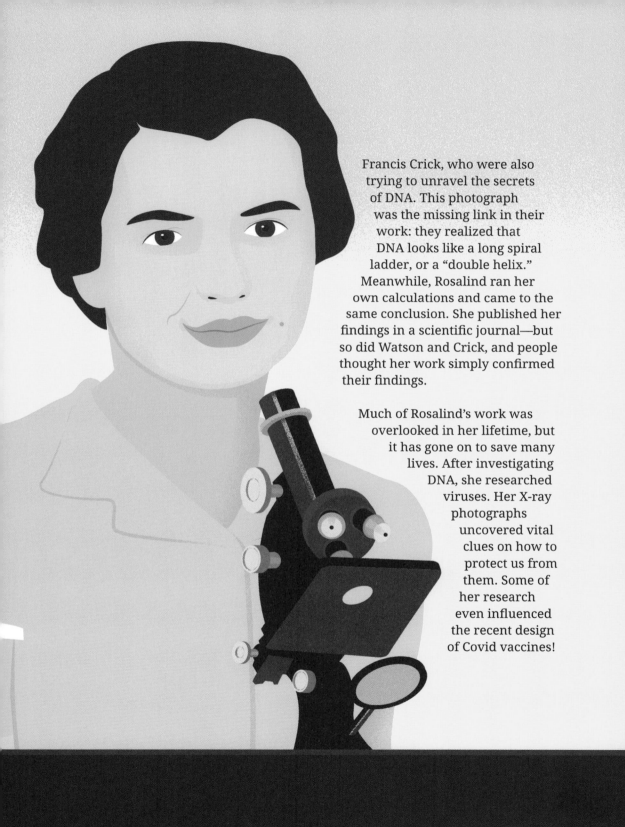

Francis Crick, who were also trying to unravel the secrets of DNA. This photograph was the missing link in their work: they realized that DNA looks like a long spiral ladder, or a "double helix." Meanwhile, Rosalind ran her own calculations and came to the same conclusion. She published her findings in a scientific journal—but so did Watson and Crick, and people thought her work simply confirmed their findings.

Much of Rosalind's work was overlooked in her lifetime, but it has gone on to save many lives. After investigating DNA, she researched viruses. Her X-ray photographs uncovered vital clues on how to protect us from them. Some of her research even influenced the recent design of Covid vaccines!

MADELINE STUART

Country: Australia | **Born:** November 13, 1996 | **Best known as:** First professional model with Down Syndrome

Models swept down the catwalk at the 2014 fashion parade in Brisbane, Australia. Madeline Stuart was struck by how glamorous they were, and she decided she wanted to be a model too. Her mother told her it wasn't going to be easy. There wasn't a single model in the world with Down syndrome. That didn't matter to Madeline: somebody has to be the first to achieve extraordinary things.

Madeline knew she had what it took to become a model. She just needed other people to believe in her too, so she shared some photos on social media. The post went viral. Millions of people saw it and thought she'd be a wonderful addition to the catwalk. Fashion brands noticed it too, and swooped in to snap her up. Madeline's first show was a big one: she dazzled at New York Fashion Week in a silver and cream dress, radiating the same confidence and beauty on the runway that she had admired in the models back home. Madeline didn't fit the profile of a typical model and she stole the show because of it. Her debut appearance was a spectacular success!

Modeling offers soon flooded in from all over the world. Magazines wanted her on their front cover and she traveled to many countries to work with the biggest fashion brands. She loves every second out on the runway, but underneath she has a more important mission. She wants to change the way people see disabilities and smash through stereotypes, one photoshoot at a time.

Madeline doesn't just wear clothes: she designs them too. Two years after her first appearance on the catwalk, she launched her own fashion label. In front of a packed audience at New York Fashion Week, she introduced the world to 21 Reasons Why. The name was cleverly chosen because she wants to educate people about Down syndrome. Inside our cells we all have chromosomes—thin strands of DNA—which tell our body how to grow. People with Down syndrome have twenty-one chromosomes rather than twenty, and Madeline is very proud of her extra one. Real life is made up of a beautiful spectrum of differences and she believes there should be no boundaries regardless of age, race, gender, or ability—and our clothes should reflect this.

SOPHIA DuLEEP SINGH

Country: UK and India | **Born:** August 8, 1876 | **Died:** August 22, 1948 |
Best known for: Suffragette who fought for women's rights in Britain and India

VOTES FOR WOMEN

Sophia Duleep Singh was a princess without a kingdom. Her father, the Maharaja of Punjab, was once head of the mighty Sikh Empire in India. But after the British took his country, the fifteen-year-old ruler was sent to live in Britain. Here he found favor with Queen Victoria, who gave him an allowance to live off. The Maharaja was very popular at the royal court and he built a great palace in the Suffolk countryside. Growing up with Queen Victoria as her godmother, Princess Sophia was a big celebrity who wore all the latest fashions and was invited to every party going. Whilst she enjoyed high society life, she was also curious about her cultural heritage. She and her sisters wanted to attend a party for King Edward VII's coronation in Delhi, but the government had forbidden her family from traveling to India. Sophia decided to go anyway.

Out in the country of her ancestors, Sophia discovered a shocking truth. Her people were suffering. Colonial rule had caused poverty, starvation, and inequality on the most devastating scale. Seeing everything that her family had lost woke something inside her.

Sophia went to India as a self-obsessed party girl and came back with a purpose. In London she heard the cries of women fighting for the right to vote and she joined them. Using her position as a princess, she called in favors and raised large sums of money. She broke the law by refusing to pay her taxes. "Why," she asked, "should I pay taxes when I have no say in how they are spent?" Her former friends didn't understand and shunned her as she stood outside her home at Hampton Court Palace selling *The Suffragette* newspaper.

On November 18, 1910, three hundred women marched on the Houses of Parliament with Sophia at the lead. The protestors were met by police, but instead of being arrested they were violently beaten. Sophia broke through the cordon and fought off a police officer who was hurting another woman. This day became known as Black Friday. When World War I broke out, women stopped their campaigning to support the war effort. Sophia turned her attention to raising funds for Indian soldiers who were fighting in the British army, often without proper equipment or clothing. She also volunteered as a nurse, caring for soldiers who had been wounded in the fighting.
In 1918, some women over the age of thirty were given the right to vote. In 1928, all women over the age of 21 could vote. Sophia could have opted for a life of parties and privilege, but instead she used her position to help change the world.

ANNA POLITKOVSKAYA

Country: Russia | **Born:** August 30, 1958 | **Died:** October 7, 2006 | **Best known as:** Investigative reporter and human rights activist

Anna Politkovskaya was not afraid of the truth. This inspired her to study journalism at university. Afterward, working for a newspaper, she got to travel around Russia and see the whole country, rather than just the privileged parts she'd known growing up. This opened her eyes to injustice, and she spent her life making others aware of social issues.

When hundreds of thousands of refugees started pouring into Russia, Anna wanted to cover their story. They came from Chechnya and were fleeing from a terrible war. Chechnya is officially part of Russia, but many of the people living there wanted to break away and become an independent country. The Russian government was not happy about this, so they sent in soldiers to stop it. The fighting was vicious, with many civilians caught in the middle. Anna was shocked by their stories. She knew she had to find out what was really going on.

In Chechnya, Anna couldn't believe what she saw. Many horrible crimes were being carried out by both sides. People in the world needed to know what was happening—so she told them. Soon, everybody had heard about the war.

Anna's reputation grew as her articles traveled far and wide. When Chechen terrorists took over a theater in Moscow, they asked for her. She walked inside alone, scared of what she would find, and did her best to negotiate the release of the hostages.

Reporting the truth was dangerous, and many people tried to silence her. Once, she was forced to run through the Chechen hills all night to avoid being arrested by Russian forces. Another time she was not so lucky and got captured. Her actions did not make her very popular with the government in Russia: they did not like her criticizing them and she fell mysteriously ill when somebody poisoned her tea. But these threats did not work and each time Anna calmly went straight back to work. In 2006, Anna was murdered. It isn't clear who was responsible.

Anna could have chosen to ignore the terrible acts of violence that were being committed, but she did not. Instead, she bravely put herself at risk so that others would know the truth. Her hope was that her actions would make a difference and create a world where everybody's human rights are respected.

SHELLY-ANN FRASER-PRYCE

Country: Jamaica | **Born:** December 27, 1986 | **Best known as:** Three-time Olympic gold medallist sprinter and third-fastest woman of all time

There were days when Shelly-Ann Fraser-Pryce didn't want to practice sprinting. She thought it was pointless to keep training because there was no way someone like her could ever strike it big. Her mother disagreed. She encouraged Shelly-Ann to keep trying, but more than anything else, she taught her to believe in herself.

Shelly-Ann grew up in a tough neighborhood in Kingston, Jamaica. With gangs on the streets and the sound of gunfire in the air, there weren't many positive role models for her to look up to. But whenever she got the chance, Shelly-Ann would run. It was her favorite thing to do and she won school competitions barefoot. Her talent was spotted by a former student who paid for her to go to secondary school and continue her training. She didn't always believe in herself, but others did and this filled her with determination to become the best in the world.

In 2008, Shelly-Ann went into the Beijing Olympic Games as an unknown and came out with a gold medal in the 100-meter race. Nobody expected her to win, but she flew out of the starting blocks and smashed her personal best, leaving her competitors far behind. This was the start of a remarkable international career that has spanned four Olympic Games and seen her bring home a haul of medals. Most of these were gold: ten World Championship wins, another gold in the 100 meters at the London 2012

"YOU DON'T GET TO DECIDE HOW YOUR STORY BEGINS, BUT YOU DO GET TO DECIDE HOW IT ENDS."

Ann is no stranger to these. An injury just before the Rio 2016 Olympics shattered her ambitions of a third consecutive gold medal. Racing in agony, she dug in deep to come away with an individual bronze medal and a team silver. A year later, she required emergency surgery when she gave birth to her son Zyon. Afterward, she wasn't allowed to lift weights for months. She worried that she might never get back in shape, but she kept working with her body and delivered an epic comeback at the 2019 World Championships, winning two gold medals.

Off the track, she's a superstar too. Sport changed Shelly-Ann's life, and she wants to help other children succeed. In 2013, she set up the Pocket Rocket Foundation, which gives scholarships to student athletes in Jamaica—just like the one she received!

Olympics, and one more in the 4 x 100-meter relay in the Tokyo 2020 Olympics.

Setbacks are an inevitable part of any journey, and Shelly-

ZHENG ZHENXIANG

Country: China | **Born:** 1929 | **Best known as:** Archaeologist who uncovered a Bronze Age tomb

When she saw the jade pendant glittering in the dirt, Zheng Zhenxiang knew she was about to make a remarkable discovery. For months she had painstakingly excavated a hillside in Anyang, China. Locals wanted to flatten the earth for farming, but Zhenxiang had uncovered some ancient building materials and believed that there was more to be found deep underground.

Many of her fellow archaeologists disagreed and told her she was wasting her time. But Zhenxiang pulled together a team to prove her theory right. Her area of expertise was the Shang Dynasty, the first ruling family in China that we know about, and she had spent many years at university studying this ancient civilization.

Zhenxiang and her team began to dig. Underneath 26 feet (8 meters) of soil they found the exquisite jade pendant, and the entrance to a tomb. It dated back to the Bronze Age and it was clear it had belonged to somebody important.

Now she faced a big challenge: the digging had disturbed the ground and water began to seep into the tomb. The archaeologists had to move quickly to make sure nothing got damaged. Carefully, they pulled thousands of precious artefacts out of the ground. There were bronze relics, jade carvings, pieces of ivory, daggers, and a large battle-ax. Sixteen skeletons lay in niches in the wall, showing that whoever put them there believed in the grisly practice of human sacrifice, which was thought to provide the dead with servants in the afterlife.

When Zhenxiang examined the inscriptions written on bones and bronze vessels she discovered that the tomb belonged to Fu Hao (also known as Lady Hao). She was one of the many wives of Wu Ding, King of the Shang Dynasty, who ruled northeast China around 1200 BCE. Fu Hao was a great warrior general and priestess, who controlled her own lands and led many military campaigns to protect her people. Once, leading 13,000 soldiers into battle, she defeated the fierce Tu-Fang tribe who had been fighting the Shang Dynasty for many years. In fact, she's thought to be the first female military leader in history.

It was a spectacular find for Zhenxiang. The tomb's location miles away from the royal cemetery had kept it safe from grave robbers. Because it hadn't been disturbed for thousands of years it helped us learn more about the Shang Dynasty and its customs, as well as the extraordinary life of Fu Hao. Zhenxiang is an incredible archaeologist who believed in herself, even when others did not, and she became known as the First Lady of Chinese Archaeology.

MAYA ANGELOU

Country: USA | **Born:** April 4, 1928 | **Died:** May 28, 2014 | **Best known as:** Award-winning author, poet, filmmaker, and civil rights activist

Words are very powerful. For many years, Maya Angelou only saw the destruction they could cause. She had a very difficult childhood and was scared that her voice would hurt others. This anxiety stopped her from speaking to anyone but her brother. Instead, she learned how to listen, and found happiness in the local library. She loved to read more than anything else and discovered that she had an incredible memory. For six years she stayed silent, until her teacher, Mrs Flowers, encouraged her to start talking again. She told Maya that poetry needs to be spoken for it to be truly understood— and she was right! The words on the page came alive when she read them out loud.

Maya's voice went on to change the world. In her first book, *I Know Why The Caged Bird Sings*, she shared the trauma she experienced and the racism she endured, bringing these serious issues to light. She refused to let her own struggles define her and encouraged others to find strength in difficult moments. Her book broke many boundaries and stayed on the bestseller list for over two years.

Sometimes, using your voice for good isn't the easiest path to take. Maya spoke up when she saw injustice, but not everyone liked what she had to say. Once, she was fired from a job for doing this. After she heard Martin Luther King Jr. speak, she became

"IF YOU'RE ALWAYS TRYING TO BE NORMAL, YOU WILL NEVER KNOW HOW AMAZING YOU CAN BE."

involved in the civil rights movement, and added her voice to the cause. Her call for equality helped people to take notice.

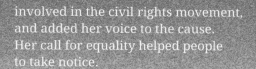

Maya's talents were endless and she didn't just excel at writing. Early in her career she worked as a dancer, an actor, and a singer, which allowed her to travel around the world. She briefly became a journalist, then a teacher, and won awards as a playwright, filmmaker, and director. However, she is best known for her vivid poetry that came straight from the heart. She read one of her poems in front of an enormous crowd when Bill Clinton was sworn in as President of the United States in 1993. This was only the second time a poet had been asked to take part in an inauguration. Throughout her incredible life, Maya found her voice and used it to drive change, and in doing so she helped others find theirs.

AUD THE DEEP-MINDED

Countries: Norway, Scotland, and Iceland | **Born and died:** Ninth century CE | **Best known as:** Early Viking settler in Iceland

Over a thousand years ago, the Vikings left their homelands in Scandinavia and sailed across the seas in longships to raid villages and plunder riches. Some of them decided to settle in the new lands they found. Aud the Deep-Minded—or Aud Ketilsdóttir, as she was known then—was born in Norway. Her life was filled with unimaginable tragedy, but she carved out a future for her family in another land.

Aud's father was a famed military commander. He had angered King Harald Fairhair, a terrible tyrant, and rather than stay in Norway and risk being slaughtered in his sleep, he took his family to live in the Scottish Hebrides. To the south of these rugged islands was Ireland, and this is where Aud married Olaf, the King of Dublin. They had a son, but when her husband was killed in battle she returned to her family in the Hebrides. Her

son, Thorstein, grew up to become a fearsome warlord who conquered large parts of Scotland. He made peace with the Scottish chieftains, but it didn't last. They plotted against him and he too was killed.

When Aud heard of her son's death, she built a large ship in secret. It was up to her to keep her grandchildren safe, and she knew it wouldn't be long before whispers of her weak position spread and the chieftains came for them too. They needed to leave before the snows thawed and it became easier for their enemies to travel.

Finally, the ship was ready and set sail, with Aud commanding twenty men who put their faith in her abilities as a leader. It also carried prisoners who had been captured and forced into slavery. They sailed west, making the treacherous journey to Iceland, an unforgiving land of ice and snow and billowing volcanoes. The ship broke into splinters as they reached the shore, but everybody survived.

In the northwest of Iceland, Aud claimed the land between two rivers and built a house for herself and her family. Today, many of the places in this area still bear the names that she gave them, like Breakfast Point, where she stopped to have breakfast, and Comb Headland, where she once lost a comb. She freed the slaves who sailed with her and gave them land to farm. In her new home, she prospered and was given the name "Deep-Minded" because of her wise decisions in times of hardship. Her family were some of the first settlers in Iceland, and stories of her bravery were written in the great sagas about important Viking families.

SONITA ALIZADEH

Countries: Afghanistan, Iran, and USA | **Born:** November 12, 1996 | **Best known as:** Rapper who uses her voice for social justice

Sonita Alizadeh kept her dreams in a notebook. She cut photos out of magazines of the places she would live and the wonders she would see, and taped them safely inside. More than anything, she wanted to be a singer. She saved the best pages for pictures of large crowds, cheering her on the center stage.

However, this was not the future that her family planned for her. They wanted Sonita to get married, and tried to find her a husband when she was ten years old. War broke out in Afghanistan

before any arrangements could be made and Sonita fled to Iran with her family. Here, she grew up as a refugee. She learned how to read and write, and cleaned bathrooms to earn extra money for her family. As she worked, she heard rappers on the radio for the first time. She couldn't understand the words, but the emotions behind them were clear. Soon, she started writing her own rap songs, sharing the pain, fear, and hope in her heart.

Many of Sonita's friends were sold into marriage: their families accepted large sums of money in return for them. When she was sixteen, her mother asked her to return to Afghanistan. They had found a man willing to pay $9,000 (£7,000) for her. If she married him, it meant her brother could afford to buy a bride of his own. Sonita refused. She had a life in Iran—and her book of dreams.

Getting into rapping wasn't easy. Many recording studios turned her away because she didn't have the right papers, or she couldn't afford their fees. They told her she was talented, but there was nothing they could do to help. Finally, somebody took a chance on her and agreed to record a song.

Sonita painted a barcode on her forehead and recorded her song "Daughters for Sale." It went viral on YouTube, spreading far beyond the borders of Iran and Afghanistan. The rest of the world heard her cry, and they listened. She won a competition and was given a music scholarship to study in the USA. This means, one day, she can marry who she likes. She knows this isn't possible for many young girls around the world and she now campaigns to end child marriage.

ADA LOVELACE

Country: UK | **Born:** December 10, 1815 | **Died:** November 27, 1852 | **Best known as:** The world's first computer programmer

Ada Lovelace wrote a computer program. What makes this extraordinary is that she did it before cars were invented or homes had electricity. She was a true visionary who defied the strict social rules and the technological limitations of the Victorian era, and her work went on to influence modern computing.

Ada's father, Lord Byron, was a very famous poet, but he was not a good husband or father. He left the family when Ada was only five weeks old, and she never saw him again. Her mother was determined that her daughter would not grow up to become a poet like her father, full of romantic ideas and stormy moods, so she sent for the best tutors to teach her math and science.

From a young age, Ada's head was bursting with different inventions. At twelve, she wanted to learn how to fly like a bird. She designed a steam-powered machine with great wings that could flap and lift her up into the air, carefully thinking about the different materials needed to build it. She wrote this all down in a book called *Flyology*.

When Ada was seventeen, she met a man named Charles Babbage at a party. She was fascinated when he unveiled a small part of his latest invention: a gigantic machine that could perform complicated mathematical calculations. Ada knew she had to learn more about this incredible device, and he agreed to teach her. Together, they worked on his next invention: a more advanced machine called the Analytical Engine. It was designed to use punch cards (paper with small holes punched into it that told the machine what to do).

Charles was only focused on calculating numbers, but Ada had a much larger vision for the machine. She thought if it was programmed with the right code, the things it could do were endless: it would be able to process letters and symbols, and even create music. Her detailed notes about how the Analytical Engine could work were published in a scientific journal. They included a sequence of step-by-step instructions that the machine could use to perform calculations: it was the world's first computer program. During her lifetime, the Analytical Engine was never finished. Charles was a difficult man to work with and he ran out of funding, so the project was shut down. Over a hundred years later it was proved that the program Ada wrote would have worked had the machine been built.

"THAT BRAIN OF MINE IS SOMETHING MORE THAN MERELY MORTAL, AS TIME WILL SHOW."

MARIA MONTESSORI

Country: Italy | **Born:** August 31, 1870 | **Died:** May 6, 1952 |
Best known as: Doctor and educator who was nominated for a Nobel Peace Prize three times

Late at night, after all the other students had gone home, Maria Montessori went back to university and studied alone. She was training to become a physician, but she was not allowed to take part in some of the lessons with the male students. Not that her classmates wanted her there anyway: they often said unkind things about her. Maria was determined to study medicine, but she faced many barriers. She even needed the Pope's help to get into university: he wrote a letter to support her application because the medical school at the University of Rome did not allow girls in at the time. Still, her persistence paid off and she became one of the first female physicians in Italy.

Working at a hospital with children with learning disabilities, Maria saw something that all the other physicians had missed—the children were playing with breadcrumbs on the floor. They were doing their best to learn from an environment with no toys, activities, or stimulation of any kind. She created a new education program and the children under her care flourished. Many passed their exams with above average scores. We can all learn, she realized, but intelligence needs to be nurtured in lots of different ways.

After this success, Maria was asked to open a school in a deprived area in Rome, where parents worked long hours and young children were left to fend for themselves. When the doors of the Children's House were opened, fifty students turned up. Instead of making children sit still, with teachers telling them what to do (and telling them off if they got it wrong!), Maria tried something new. Every child chose what they wanted to learn and developed skills at their own pace. They learned lots of practical things—like how to serve dinner—as well as how to read and write, and soon everybody in the class was working together and eager to learn more.

During World War II, Maria had to leave Italy because she refused to let her schools be turned into training centers for young soldiers. This went against everything she believed in, so she and her son fled to Spain, then India, and finally settled in the Netherlands. They continued Maria's work, training many new teachers. Today Montessori schools are found all over the world, teaching children to be independent and confident in themselves.

"THE GREATEST GIFTS WE CAN GIVE OUR CHILDREN ARE THE ROOTS OF RESPONSIBILITY AND THE WINGS OF INDEPENDENCE."

ABOUT THE AUTHOR:
DANIELLE BROWN

Born: April 10, 1988 | **Country:** UK | **Best Achievement:** Two Paralympic gold medals and five time World Champion

Danielle wasn't naturally gifted at sport when she was younger. Her sisters used to beat her at running and swimming, and when she tried kayaking she spent more time splashing around in the water than canoeing. This didn't matter because sport was a way to have fun, meet friends, and stay active. Never, for one second, did she think it could become a career.

At eleven-years-old Danielle's feet started to hurt. It wasn't a big deal to start with, but the pain got worse. Soon she was struggling to walk and five years later she was diagnosed with a disability called Complex Regional Pain Syndrome. It was hard being unable to take part in the sports she loved, so she started to look for something that didn't involve running or walking—and that's how she discovered archery.

Danielle wasn't very good at archery when she first tried it: she spent most of her time picking arrows off the ground not the target, but it was so much fun and she wanted to practice all the time. Three years later she made the Great Britain team. She jumped straight in as World Number One and held this position for the rest of her international career.

At the Beijing 2008 Paralympic Games she started the competition with a World Record. It was all looking great, but the night before the semi-finals she felt anxious. What if she couldn't do it tomorrow? After reading inspirational words from her support team, Danielle went out and delivered big results. Beating both opponents by a convincing margin, she took gold. She also learned that if she wanted to keep winning she had to believe in herself and her ability no matter what. When she got home Danielle spent a lot of time working on her confidence levels. As her confidence increased, so did her results. World records, world firsts, world titles, and another gold medal in front of the home crowd in London 2012. She is also the first disabled athlete to represent England on the able-bodied team: at the 2010 Commonwealth Games she won a gold medal in the team event.

Danielle believes that we can all achieve big things when given the right encouragement and support. She's very passionate about making sure that girls and disabled people all over the world can access opportunities.

"EVEN IN ADVERSITY WE HAVE A CHOICE— TO GET UP OR TO GIVE UP."

INDEX

A

acting 67, 70
Alizadeh, Sonita 102–103
Alonso, Alicia 46–47
Angelou, Maya 98–99
Anning, Mary 26–27
archaeology 97
architecture 62, 63
Ardern, Jacinda 74–75
Artemisia I of Caria 42–43
art 8, 16, 80, 88, 103
Arzner, Dorothy 80–81
astrology 12, 13
astronomy 10
athletics 22, 23, 53, 82, 83, 94, 95, 108
Aud the Deep-Minded 100–101
aviation 14, 15, 76, 77

B

Beyoncé 16–17
Bly, Nellie 18–19
Boudicca 24–25
Braille 50
Brown, Danielle 108–109
business 56, 57, 88

C

civil rights 19, 20, 98, 99
Cleopatra 72–73
Clooney, Amal 84–85
conservation 44, 45, 49, 60
Cristoforetti, Samantha 76–77
Curie, Marie 28–29

D

dance 16, 46
De Jongh, Andrée 68–69

De Pizan, Christine 12–13

E

Earhart, Amelia 14–15
education 39, 44, 45, 58, 67, 78, 106
Eliot, George 36–37
empowerment 13, 16, 73, 75, 82, 83, 108
entrepreneurship 26, 27, 56, 57, 88
environment 49, 60
equality 20, 21, 30, 35, 41, 49, 50, 56, 57,
    84, 91, 92

F

fashion 88
feminism 16, 39, 41, 49, 50, 67, 70, 78, 91
Finnbogadóttir, Vigdís 34–35
Fonda, Jane 70–71
Franklin, Rosalind 86–87
Fraser-Pryce, Shelley-Ann 94–95

G

Gacio, Susana Rodríguez 52–53
gender equality 41, 67, 78, 91
Ginsburg, Ruth Bader 40–41
Goodall, Jane 44–45

H

Hadid, Zaha 62–63
Hypatia 10–11

I

inventions 28, 29, 54, 56, 57, 80, 104

J

journalism 19, 92
justice 30, 41, 84, 103

K

Kahlo, Frida 8–9
Keller, Helen 50–51
Kom, Mary 82–83
Kosmala, Libby 22–23

L

law 40, 84
leadership 24, 32, 33, 35, 42, 73, 75, 100, 101
Lovelace, Ada 104–105

M

Maathai, Wangari 48–49
math 10, 104
Meitner, Lise 54–55
mental health 19, 98, 99, 108
Montessori, Maria 106–107
movies 70, 80
music 16, 103

N

Nightingale, Florence 58–59
nursing 14, 58, 68

P

palaeontology 26
paralympics 22, 23, 53, 108
Parks, Rosa 20–21
Patten, Mary 64–65
philanthropy 39, 44, 45, 56, 57, 84
philosophy 10, 78
piracy 33
poetry 13, 98, 99
politics 35, 75, 78
Politkovskaya, Anna 92–93

R

racism 19, 20, 98, 99
record-breaking 14, 16, 35, 53, 62, 63, 64, 75, 108
Rickard, Tuaiwa "Eva" 30–32

S

science 26, 27, 28, 29, 44, 45, 54, 76, 77, 86, 87, 96, 97
segregation 20, 21
Shih, Ching 32–33
Singh, Sophia Duleep 90–91
singing 16, 103
social change 20, 21, 30, 41, 60, 75, 91, 92, 98, 99, 103
spaceflight 76, 77
sport 22, 23, 53, 82, 83, 94, 95, 108
Stuart, Madeline 88–89

T

teaching 10, 41, 44, 45, 46, 54, 80, 106
Thunberg, Greta 60–61

V, W

voting rights 50, 91
Walker, Madam C. J. 56–57
war 24, 32, 33, 42, 68, 70
Watson, Emma 66–67
Wollstonecraft, Mary 78–79
women's rights 39, 49, 67, 70, 78
writing 13, 14, 19, 36, 39, 50, 58, 78, 98, 99, 104

Y, Z

Yousafzai, Malala 38–39
Zhenxiang, Zheng 96–97

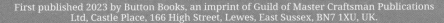

First published 2023 by Button Books, an imprint of Guild of Master Craftsman Publications Ltd, Castle Place, 166 High Street, Lewes, East Sussex, BN7 1XU, UK.

Text © Danielle Brown, 2023.
Copyright in the Work @ GMC Publications Ltd, 2023

ISBN: 978 1 78708 139 0

Distributed by Publishers Group West in the United States.

A catalog record for this book is available from the British Library.

Publisher: Jonathan Bailey
Production Director: Jim Bulley
Senior Project Editor: Susie Behar
Design & Illustration: Robin Shields and Emily Hurlock
Editor: Claire Saunders
Publishing Assistant: Charlotte Mockridge

Color origination by GMC Reprographics.

Printed and bound in China.

For more on Button Books, contact:
GMC Publications Ltd, Castle Place,
166 High Street, Lewes, East Sussex,
BN7 1XU, United Kingdom
Tel: +44 (0)1273 488005
buttonbooks.co.uk
buttonbooks.us

Button Books

FSC
www.fsc.org
MIX
Paper | Supporting responsible forestry
FSC® C144853

MUSICIAN JOURNALIST ACTIVIST PARALYMPIAN
SIDENT JUDGE COMMANDER CONSERVATIONIST
SWOMAN NURSE ARCHITECT ACTRESS PHARAOH
TOR BOXER LAWYER CHEMIST MODEL REPORTER
DOCTOR ARTIST MATHEMATICIAN ASTRONOMER
RALYMPIAN QUEEN PALEONTOLOGIST SCIENTIST
SERVATIONIST BALLERINA CHOREOGRAPHER
TRESS PHARAOH PRIME MINISTER ASTRONAUT
MODEL REPORTER OLYMPIAN ARCHAEOLOGIST
CIAN ASTRONOMER WRITER PILOT MUSICIAN
LEONTOLOGIST SCIENTIST PIRATE PRESIDENT
CHOREOGRAPHER PHYSICIST BUSINESSWOMAN
NISTER ASTRONAUT PHILOSOPHER DIRECTOR
AN ARCHAEOLOGIST POET PROGRAMMER DOCTOR
R PILOT MUSICIAN JOURNALIST ACTIVIST
IST PIRATE PRESIDENT JUDGE COMMANDER
HYSICIST BUSINESSWOMAN NURSE ARCHITECT
T PHILOSOPHER DIRECTOR BOXER LAWYER
LOGIST POET PROGRAMMER DOCTOR ARTIST
SICIAN JOURNALIST ACTIVIST PARALYMPIAN
SIDENT JUDGE COMMANDER CONSERVATIONIST
SWOMAN NURSE ARCHITECT ACTRESS PHARAOH
TOR BOXER LAWYER CHEMIST MODEL REPORTER
DOCTOR ARTIST MATHEMATICIAN ASTRONOMER
RALYMPIAN QUEEN PALEONTOLOGIST SCIENTIST

ARTIST MATHEMATICIAN ASTRONOMER WRITER P
QUEEN PALEONTOLOGIST SCIENTIST PIRATE P
BALLERINA CHOREOGRAPHER PHYSICIST BUSIN
PRIME MINISTER ASTRONAUT PHILOSOPHER DIR
OLYMPIAN ARCHAEOLOGIST POET PROGRAMME
WRITER PILOT MUSICIAN JOURNALIST ACTIVIST
PIRATE PRESIDENT JUDGE COMMANDER C
PHYSICIST BUSINESSWOMAN NURSE ARCHITECT
PHILOSOPHER DIRECTOR BOXER LAWYER CHEM
POET PROGRAMMER DOCTOR ARTIST MATHEM
JOURNALIST ACTIVIST PARALYMPIAN QUEEN
JUDGE COMMANDER CONSERVATIONIST BALLER
NURSE ARCHITECT ACTRESS PHARAOH PRIME
BOXER LAWYER CHEMIST MODEL REPORTER OLY
ARTIST MATHEMATICIAN ASTRONOMER WR
PARALYMPIAN QUEEN PALEONTOLOGIST SCI
CONSERVATIONIST BALLERINA CHOREOGRAPHE
ACTRESS PHARAOH PRIME MINISTER ASTRO
CHEMIST MODEL REPORTER OLYMPIAN ARCH
MATHEMATICIAN ASTRONOMER WRITER PILOT
QUEEN PALEONTOLOGIST SCIENTIST PIRATE P
BALLERINA CHOREOGRAPHER PHYSICIST BUSIN
PRIME MINISTER ASTRONAUT PHILOSOPHER DIR
OLYMPIAN ARCHAEOLOGIST POET PROGRAMME
WRITER PILOT MUSICIAN JOURNALIST ACTIVIST
PIRATE PRESIDENT JUDGE COMMANDER